"In *Teaching and Learning for Intercultural Understanding: E*
Rader has produced a clearly structured, carefully re
encourages its readers to integrate intercultural understa..
lenges them to reflect on issues relating to their own cultures, beliefs, v...
new title promises to be a must-read for anyone with a concern for supporting the young a..
of tomorrow in developing the skills and attributes that will be essential if they are to live peacefully with others in our increasingly complex world."

   — *Mary Hayden, Professor of International Education, University of Bath, UK*

"Indispensable reading for teachers today. This is a remarkable book, perhaps even a courageous
one. Debra Rader's appeal to teachers blends theory and practice into a narrative that is passionate
and inspiring, urgent and compelling, with a mine of resources and ideas for lessons and activities.
It will be a seminal text on how to address the most important educational challenge of our era."

   — *Terry Haywood, Trustee, Alliance for International Education and*
International Schools Consultant

"Debra Rader's book is a deep dive into what intercultural understanding is, why it is vital to our
global wellbeing, and how to foster it in children. Approachable, insightful, practical, and hopeful, it is
a must-have resource for educators committed to making the world a better place, one child at a time."

   — *Rana DiOrio, author of the award-winning* 'What Does It Mean to Be . . .?®'
children's picture book series

"Digitalisation has connected people, countries and continents, bringing together a majority
of the world's population in ways that vastly increases our individual and collective potential.
But the same forces have also made the world more volatile, more complex and more uncertain. More than ever, schools are called to help students see the world through different eyes,
appreciate different cultures and divergent thinking, and to build a shared understanding among
groups with diverse experiences and interests, thus increasing our radius of trust to strangers and
institutions. This is easy to say, but really hard to accomplish in a classroom. This book provides
a framework for how to do this, and not only that, it also illustrates in insightful and practical
ways what it might look like when intercultural understanding is lived in our daily lives."

   — *Andreas Schleicher, Director, OECD Directorate for Education and Skills, and*
Special Advisor on Education Policy to the Secretary-General

"This book is an excellent resource for the multicultural and multilingual children I teach. The
literature recommendations are diverse, relevant to my students' lives, and consistently provide
opportunities for meaningful conversations. The lesson plans have been transformative for all
the students in my class, and have deepened their appreciation of and thirst to learn more about
all cultures and languages. Through this learning, my entire class raised their awareness of how
we can honor our differences, engage with one another respectfully, and each help make the
world a better place."

   — *Grace Friedman, Fifth grade teacher at White Center Heights*
Elementary School, Seattle, WA, USA

"*Teaching and Learning for Intercultural Understanding* is a critical exploration on how, as educators,
we can intentionally build the values and skills children need to engage positively in an ever-
increasing intercultural world. The rich array of quality children's literature featured, and the
thoughtful and well-developed lesson plans that Ms. Rader has created to support the development of these essential skills offer valuable practical application for the classroom. Teachers will
love them!"

   —*Julia Alden, International School Leader and Educator*

"With this thoughtful book, Debra Rader has given primary schools the gift of the '*what*', '*why*' and '*how*' of intercultural understanding. Whereas previous experiences in developing intercultural understanding at the primary level may have been limited to food, flags and festivals, Rader's framework provides us with components of intercultural understanding and language with which to dialogue about it. This language is particularly helpful as we begin to think of ways to assess intercultural understanding. Based on current research, Rader also provides us with meaningful suggestions and activities that will allow all of us to integrate the development of intercultural understanding in our programs – rather than having it as an "add on" to our curriculum. This book serves as a very useful tool to extend the emotional intelligence of teachers."

— *Ochan Kusuma-Powell, co-author of* 'Becoming an Emotionally
Intelligent Teacher'

"The power of intercultural understanding! This book could not have appeared at a better time. It does more than offer a clear and easy-to-read exploration of intercultural understanding, a topic that matters in our changing, challenging and uncertain world. The researched-based guidelines will support teachers as they guide young children and help them understand and learn from the diversity they see around them. The many examples, strategies and activities will help children develop accepting and positive attitudes towards the many ways people live, speak, dress, eat, worship and celebrate. The author provides a framework for developing intercultural understanding and invites teachers to integrate it into their prescribed curricula, connect their teaching to children's lives and transform their classrooms into exciting multicultural and multilingual places."

— *Roma Chumak-Horbatsch, Associate Professor School of Early
Childhood Studies, Ryerson University, Canada*

"Debra Rader has written an invaluable and comprehensive resource for educators to support the development of intercultural understanding in the children they teach. Both new and veteran teachers will find a rich treasure trove of activities and literature that can be easily woven into any existing curriculum. An impressive work!"

— *Mary Hannert, Early Childhood Educator, St Paul, USA*

"Debra Rader makes a strong case for including teaching and learning for intercultural understanding into the school curriculum of young learners. Based on both thorough research and her own hands-on experiences, she clearly and passionately offers ideas as to how teachers can encourage and nurture intercultural understanding through rich discussions, meaningful activities, and detailed lesson plans based on quality children's literature. In addition, readers have a chance to reflect on their own understanding of the topics as they "pause for reflection" at various points along their journey through this most important book. A must-read for all teachers as they strive to teach compassion, and appreciation and understanding of both their own cultures and traditions and those of others."

— *Sally Ott, Former Lower School Principal, The Latin School of Chicago, USA*

"Debra Rader takes us on a guided journey addressing a wide range of developmentally appropriate tasks aimed at helping young learners enhance their intercultural sensitivity, knowledge and skills. This book presents a comprehensive theoretical underpinning of the oftentimes-abstract concepts and critical issues related to intercultural development in concrete and tangible ways, laying a foundation for the wide range of practical strategies included in each chapter. This book is a welcomed and needed contribution for teachers concerned with enhancing the intercultural development of young children."

— *Kenneth Cushner, Emeritus Professor of International and Intercultural
Education, Kent State University, USA*

Teaching and Learning for Intercultural Understanding

Teaching and Learning for Intercultural Understanding is a comprehensive resource for educators in primary and early years classrooms. It provides teachers with a complete framework for developing intercultural understanding among pupils and includes practical and creative strategies and activities to stimulate discussion, awareness and comprehension of intercultural issues and ideas.

Drawing on the most current research and work in the field of intercultural competence and existing models of intercultural understanding, this book explores topics such as:

- understanding culture and language
- the importance of personal and cultural identity
- engaging with difference
- cultivating positive attitudes and beliefs
- embedding awareness of local and global issues in students
- designing a classroom with intercultural understanding in mind.

With detailed ready-to-use, enquiry-based lesson plans, which incorporate children's literature, talking points and media resources, this book encourages the practitioner to consider intercultural understanding as another lens through which to view the curriculum when creating and choosing learning materials and activities. *Teaching and Learning for Intercultural Understanding* sets out to help the reader engage young hearts and minds with global and local concepts in a way that is easily integrated into the life of all primary schools – from New York to New Delhi, from Birmingham to Bangkok.

Debra Rader is a former primary school headteacher with over 30 years' experience teaching and working with children and families from multicultural and multilingual backgrounds. She is an international educational consultant and develops programmes and workshops linked to intercultural understanding.

Teaching and Learning for Intercultural Understanding

Engaging Young Hearts and Minds

Debra Rader

Routledge
Taylor & Francis Group

LONDON AND NEW YORK

First published 2018
by Routledge
2 Park Square, Milton Park, Abingdon, Oxon OX14 4RN

and by Routledge
711 Third Avenue, New York, NY 10017

Routledge is an imprint of the Taylor & Francis Group, an informa business

British Library Cataloguing in Publication Data
A catalogue record for this book is available from the British Library

Library of Congress Cataloging in Publication Data
Names: Rader, Debra, author.
Title: Teaching and learning for intercultural understanding :
    engaging young hearts and minds / Debra Rader.
Description: Abingdon, Oxon ; New York, NY : Routledge, 2018. |
    Includes bibliographical references.
Identifiers: LCCN 2017059073 (print) | LCCN 2018012669
    (ebook) | ISBN 9781138102712 (hbk) | ISBN
    9781138102729 (pbk) | ISBN 9781315103495 (ebk)
Subjects: LCSH: Multiculturalism—Study and teaching (Early
    childhood) | Multiculturalism—Study and teaching (Primary)
    | Multiculturalism—Study and teaching—Activity programs.
Classification: LCC LC1099 (ebook) | LCC LC1099 .R33 2018
    (print) | DDC 370.117—dc23
LC record available at https://lccn.loc.gov/2017059073

ISBN: 978-1-138-10271-2 (hbk)
ISBN: 978-1-138-10272-9 (pbk)
ISBN: 978-1-315-10349-5 (ebk)

Typeset in Bembo
by Swales & Willis Ltd, Exeter, Devon, UK

Acknowledgements

The writing of this book has truly been an emotional, spiritual and intellectual journey.

I am grateful to all of the children, families, friends and colleagues I have had the privilege of knowing and working with who have enriched my life through their diversity, and continue to deepen and expand my own intercultural understanding.

I would like to thank Bob Tracy for his invaluable feedback on the manuscript. I admire his deeply held belief in human rights and his commitment to social advocacy. I am grateful for his valued friendship and expertise.

I express my deepest thanks to Mary Hannert and Sally Ott for their educational expertise, enduring friendship, and enormous enthusiasm and support. The time they devoted to reading the manuscript and the feedback they provided contributed greatly to this book.

I would like to thank Julia Alden for her recognition of the importance of this work and its place in our world, and for her valued comments on drafts of the work.

Thank you to Barbara Reeves for her helpful feedback and enthusiastic support, particularly in the early stages of this project.

Many thanks to Dr Kenneth Cushner for sharing resources, for his valuable insights and experience, and for his leadership in the field of intercultural education.

As always Richard Pearce provided inspired conversation, and I thank him for his encouragement and belief in the work.

Special thanks to Saskia Pauwels and Linda Erickson for reading through drafts and providing valuable feedback and encouragement.

I would like to thank children's librarian, Patricia Cohn, for sharing her knowledge and love of children's literature.

Much appreciation to Maggie Hos-McGrane for her support in highlighting teaching and learning for intercultural understanding at ASB, and for sharing her tremendous ICT expertise.

I wish to extend my heartfelt thanks to the outstanding educators whose contributions and examples of teaching and learning for intercultural understanding enrich this book. They include: Darlene Huson, Primary Principal, AISL, and educator Chye de Ryckel; John Smithies, Elementary School Principal, ASB, and educators Tracy Blair and Andrew Marama; Jenny O'Fee, Primary School Principal, BMS; educators at ISD, Ana Tetley and Julie Tyler; Sarah Kupke, Head of Campus, ISS Sindelfingen and her colleagues, Amanda Haworth, Elke Clarus and Owen Murphy; Maria Menelao, educator at La Scuola Primaria di Monte San Quirico; Jo Wheeler, Principal, Westgarth Primary School; Susan Stanford, Principal, Thornwood Public School, and educator Safia Shere; educator Grace Friedman at White Center Heights Elementary School; and educators Jeffrey Brewster and Miles Madison.

I am deeply appreciative of all of the educators, researchers, and organisations around the world who work towards helping to create a more peaceful, equitable and compassionate world, and to all of you who also believe deeply in children, and in bringing teaching and learning for intercultural understanding into our schools.

Many thanks to my family, friends and colleagues who have shared in my passion in writing this book and encouraged its development. I am particularly grateful for the enormous love and support from Sara MacDonald and Arleen Johnson. I thank Anna Albright for her love and wisdom, and for her steadfast belief in this work.

I would like to express my deepest thanks to Bruce Roberts, Alice Gray and the team at Routledge for their vision and support of this important and timely subject.

Finally I would like to thank my husband, Jim Kachenmeister, for reading and providing feedback on the many drafts, for his love and patience, and for his unwavering belief in the value of this work.

General tips

- Be mindful of instilling the value of doing good for its intrinsic value, rather than for external recognition. Consider service learning projects that value and include human relationships and do not rely solely on raising funds.

- The use of technology in schools is exciting and provides numerous opportunities for learning. I also believe there is great value in non-digital student created materials. Children need to develop a range of skills, and I advocate a blend of pencil/paper tasks and organically created projects alongside the use of technology.

- Have the confidence and courage to enter into challenging discussions with students, parents and colleagues. It is fine to admit you do not know, or need to think about the topic or situation more. Seek support from your professional colleagues and resources from the community at large.

- Recognise the challenge of achieving the delicate balance between raising awareness of very real and important intercultural and global issues with children, and also preserving the joy and magic of childhood.

Compelling pedagogy for our times

Within the Australian Curriculum, intercultural understanding is developed around three organising elements:

- Recognising culture and developing respect
    Students: Investigate culture and cultural identity
            Explore and compare cultural knowledge, beliefs and practices
            Develop respect for cultural diversity

- Interacting and empathising with others
    Students: Communicate across cultures
            Consider and develop multiple perspectives
            Empathise with others

- Reflecting on intercultural experiences and taking responsibility
    Students: Reflect on intercultural experiences
            Challenge stereotypes and prejudices
            Mediate cultural difference

(ACARA, 2011)

I have found that the Australian Curriculum has clearly identified the key aspects of intercultural understanding and distilled its essence. The knowledge, skills, values and attitudes embedded here form an excellent foundation to expand upon.

UNESCO has also published a highly useful document, *Education for Intercultural Understanding* (de Leo, 2010), for teaching and learning for intercultural understanding. It includes suggested learning outcomes that develop content, values and skills, and provides suggestions for integrating intercultural understanding across the curriculum and creating an atmosphere conducive to developing intercultural understanding.

Intercultural competence

Like intercultural understanding, the term *intercultural competence* has been widely used, discussed and debated, and does also not have a fully agreed upon definition. Dr Kenneth Cushner, former Professor of Multicultural and International Education at Kent State University, and a keynote speaker at the AIE Conference in Mumbai, addressed the need to nurture intercultural competence, which includes intercultural understanding and skills, in young people. He describes intercultural competence as, 'an expanded repertoire of culturally appropriate behaviour that enables the individual to interact effectively and appropriately with people different from themselves' (ISJ, April 2015).

Janet Bennett (2011) describes intercultural competence as, 'a set of cognitive, affective and behavioral skills and characteristics that support effective and appropriate interaction in a variety of cultural contexts'. They include the following:

Cognitive skills

Cultural-self awareness

Culture-general knowledge

Culture-specific knowledge

Interaction analysis

Affective skills

Curiosity

Cognitive flexibility

Motivation

Open-mindedness

Behavioural skills

Relationship building skills

Behavioural skills: listening, problem-solving

Empathy

Information gathering skills

Bhawuk and Brislin (1992) and Deardorff (2009) describe interculturally competent individuals as:

- open-minded and genuinely interested in other cultures
- observant and knowledgeable about cultural difference and similarities
- having an ability to resist stereotypes and anticipate complexity in intercultural interactions
- being able and willing to modify their behavior so they can interact and communicate effectively with those who are different from themselves.

These models suggest essential knowledge, skills and attitudes needed to interact effectively in diverse cultural settings and with others who are culturally diverse.

In *Intercultural Competences* (2011), Deardorff summarises five regional reports. Her final list of skills and competences is thought to be the minimum requirement to attain intercultural competences (cited in UNESCO, 2013). They include: Respect; Self-awareness/identity; Seeing from other perspectives/world views; Listening; Adaptation; Relationship building; and Cultural humility. I particularly like the way listening and cultural humility are highlighted in this list, as developing effective listening skills is essential for engaging in constructive dialogue and cultural humility underscores the belief that all cultures and languages have equal value: this is a critical aspect of human rights for everyone.

International-mindedness

The concept of international-mindedness is central to the IB programmes.

The IB Learner Profile states that, 'the aim of all IB programmes is to develop *internationally minded people* who, recognizing their common humanity and shared guardianship of the planet, help to create a better and more peaceful world'. This is achieved through developing the following ten attributes. IB learners strive to be: Inquirers, Knowledgeable, Thinkers, Communicators, Principled, Open-minded, Caring, Risk-takers, Balanced and Reflective.

In addition to the Learner Profile, the Attitudes promoted in the IBPYP framework are equally important to nurture and develop for intercultural understanding and international-mindedness. They include Appreciation, Commitment, Confidence, Cooperation, Creativity, Curiosity, Empathy, Enthusiasm, Independence, Integrity, Respect and Tolerance.

The results of this assessment will likely inform educational policy and inspire innovative pedagogical approaches to global competence education.

You can read more about the PISA assessment here: www.oecd.org/education/Global-competency-for-an-inclusive-world.pdf

A framework for developing intercultural understanding

As we can see, significant work has been done in intercultural understanding and related fields, and each of these models presents important elements. However, I have not found one model that I believe comprehensively includes the knowledge and understanding, beliefs, values and attitudes, skills and behaviours that are intrinsic to teaching and learning for intercultural understanding, and developing this essential disposition. This has led me to create the framework that follows.

Drawing on the breadth of valuable work in the fields of intercultural understanding, intercultural competence, cultural intelligence, international-mindedness, global citizenship and global competence, I have created a framework that synthesises and extends the common features I have found. This framework reflects the knowledge, skills, values and attitudes, and common learning outcomes I have identified and expands on them.

It includes the following four components we need to address for teaching and learning for intercultural understanding in our schools:

- Knowledge and Understanding
- Transformative Beliefs, Values and Attitudes
- Essential Intercultural, Interpersonal and Life Skills
- Engagement in Positive Action

Intercultural understanding is an essential part of living, learning and working with others in a diverse, interconnected and interdependent world. It has traditionally been addressed in foreign language classes – however, it is not only appropriate, but essential, to embed intercultural understanding in the fabric of all we do in schools and school life. Intercultural understanding and learning have also largely been focused on acquiring content knowledge and much less on developing the values and attitudes that lead to changes in behaviour. Teaching and learning for intercultural understanding is much about transforming both hearts and minds and includes learning in all three domains: cognitive, affective and behavioural. It also requires explicit teaching, modelling and practise of intercultural, interpersonal and life skills in order to live our values and attitudes and apply our knowledge and understanding in diverse cultural contexts.

Put simply, I would describe intercultural understanding as the willingness and ability to interact effectively and appropriately with people different from ourselves, and in diverse cultural settings. This requires knowledge and understanding, beliefs, values and attitudes, and skills and behaviours that are developed throughout our lives.

Framework for Developing Intercultural Understanding (Rader, 2016)

KNOWLEDGE AND UNDERSTANDING	TRANSFORMATIVE BELIEFS, VALUES AND ATTITUDES
What culture is, how it is learned and experienced	Appreciation and respect for diversity
Different cultures, cultural traits and languages	Compassion and empathy, for all and the environment
Similarities and differences between cultures	Caring and kindness
Personal and cultural identity, self and others	Open-mindedness
Self-esteem and self-confidence	Curiosity, interest in others
Link between language and culture	Tolerance and respect for difference
Cultural and linguistic diversity and its value	Belief in human rights and dignity for all
Importance of home languages	Optimism, belief we can make a positive difference
Beliefs; secular and faith-based	Responsibility for self, others and the environment
Global issues and our shared responsibility to address them	Confidence and courage
These are addressed in Chapters 4, 5 and 9.	Belief in social justice and equity
	These are addressed in Chapters 6, 7 and 9.
ESSENTIAL INTERCULTURAL, INTERPERSONAL AND LIFE SKILLS	ENGAGEMENT IN POSITIVE ACTION
Intercultural awareness and sensitivity	Put into practice what we are learning and align our beliefs and values with the way we live our lives
Communication (verbal and non-verbal)	
Consider and develop multiple perspectives	Make a positive contribution to our world, locally and globally
Develop and sustain positive relationships across cultures	Work towards a more peaceful, just and sustainable world
Recognise, challenge and resist stereotypes, prejudice, discrimination and racism	**All of the chapters lead to Engagement in Positive Action, particularly the learning outcomes in Chapters 4–9.**
Adapt, modify thinking and behaviour	
Engage in reflection; intercultural, self and others	
Creative and critical thinking	
Problem-solving and decision-making	
Collaboration and cooperation	
Peaceful conflict resolution and mediation	
Self-monitoring and self-management	
Build resilience and manage change	
These are addressed in Chapters 7 and 8.	

And the third is to leave the world a better place than you found it. My parents were avid hikers and met in a hiking club in New York City. At weekends we often escaped the city for the green of the Adirondack Mountains. It was there that I first learned about leaving the hiking trail and campsite cleaner than you found it. This carried over into trying to make a positive contribution, large or small, wherever I am.

Mobility was and has been a prominent feature of my life. We moved often, and as a child I began to learn how to build resilience and manage change. I continued to move often as an adult and have lived in six states and in London twice before moving to Lucca, Italy, where I live now. As a result I feel a bit like a New Yorker, a bit like a Londoner and a bit Lucchese. I am able to move easily between these three cultures and their languages, and feel equally at home in these three countries. I enjoy travel and welcome new cultural experiences.

PAUSE FOR REFLECTION

What is your personal story?

What cultures, languages and life experiences have shaped your life?

What values have been influential?

How did you come to the teaching profession?

My passion for education began when I was a young child. With a chalkboard attached to the back of my bedroom door, and an innate love of learning, I spent countless hours educating my imaginary class. Family gatherings at my grandparents' house inevitably turned to 'playing school' with my cousins. I was always the teacher. My grandfather was a notary public and elaborate report cards were made with an assortment of stickers and stamps. When I became a teacher it was no surprise to anyone in my family, and for me it was a true calling. It was and remains an absolute joy.

Teaching for me, like for all of us, carries enormous responsibility as well; not only to promote students' learning but also their well-being. I quickly became well aware of the profound impact teachers can have on the lives of children, both positive and negative. We have the capacity to lift their spirits and help instill self-belief, and we can inadvertently quash their spirit and foster self-doubt. I realised that I was the topic of many a dinnertime conversation in children's homes and that what I had said in the classroom was the 'inarguable truth' as parents often relayed stories of 'wise words' that I had shared.

PAUSE FOR REFLECTION

What brought you to the teaching profession?

Has that desire been met, and how?

What is it about teaching that engages your heart and brings you joy?

Knowing ourselves: the DMIS

Dr Milton Bennett developed the Developmental Model of Intercultural Sensitivity (DMIS) (1993) as a framework to explain how people experience and engage with cultural difference. It consists of six stages that fall along a continuum from an *ethnocentric* or monocultural mindset to an *ethnorelative* or intercultural mindset. As individuals move further along the continuum they are better able to exercise intercultural sensitivity.

There are six stages: *Denial, Defense, Minimization, Acceptance, Adaptation and Integration*

Denial: In the denial stage individuals do not perceive that cultural differences exist. They experience physical and/or psychological isolation from cultural difference and are disinterested in or even dismissive of intercultural communication.

Defense: People in this stage are threatened by cultural difference and tend to be highly critical of other cultures, seeing them in stereotypic or polarised ways. Cultures are perceived as 'us' and 'them' with 'us' seen as superior.

Minimization: In this stage people perceive their own cultural worldview as universal. People assume that their own physical or psychological experiences are shared by people in all cultures, and that our basic values and beliefs are essentially the same.

Acceptance: In this stage individuals recognise that their culture is just one of many worldviews. They are curious about and respectful towards cultural differences, but their knowledge of other cultures does not yet allow them to easily adapt their behaviour to different cultural contexts.

Adaptation: In this stage people are empathetic towards different cultures and can communicate and interact authentically across cultures. They have the competence to adapt their behaviour appropriately to different cultural contexts.

Integration: In this stage people can move comfortably between cultures and different worldviews. They are able to bridge cultures and mediate across cultures.

Denial, Defense and Minimization are *ethnocentric* stages and Acceptance, Adaptation and Integration are *ethnorelative* stages.

The Intercultural Development Inventory (IDI) (Hammer and Bennett, 2003) was developed to measure where along the DMIS an individual or organisation lies. It is necessary to take the IDI to find out where you actually fall on the continuum. However, I think it is a worthy exercise to consider where you would place yourself on the continuum at present.

PAUSE FOR REFLECTION

Where do you think you might fall on the DMIS continuum?

How could you move further along?

Where do you think your school lies on the continuum?

How could it move further along the continuum?

Recognising our own stereotypes and prejudice

We all hold stereotypes and prejudice, and I encourage you to have compassion and understanding for yourself as you reflect on your personal beliefs. As children we learned stereotypes and prejudice from our families, other children and the media. However, we can learn how to recognise them, challenge them and resist them.

When I was a child we used to go to La Guardia Airport in New York City to watch the planes take off and land. It was a thrill to see these jets lift off and we watched in awe as they gracefully touched down. I love airports for a whole host of reasons: for the excitement that travel brings, the opportunity to meet new people, and the way my travel experiences continually help me to be aware of my stereotypes and challenge them. I used to be completely unaware of the stream of consciousness thoughts that went through my head as I observed other passengers and made assumptions about where they were from, their possible occupation, background and social status. When I engaged in conversation I was invariably surprised to find out that their lives were very different than I had imagined. More often than not there were lovely connections made and we both walked away feeling pleased with the exchange. I now continue to observe others closely yet refrain from assuming who they are but enter into a conversation to find out. I do the same with New York City taxi drivers, who have amazing stories to tell. They are some of the most well-informed and well-educated men and women I have met, and I now know not to make assumptions but to engage with and learn about them.

We are all learning to see beyond colour and appearances to the hearts and minds that live within the human diversity we encounter. We must be aware of the stereotypes we all hold, and truly believe in the potential of each child regardless of race, ethnicity, socioeconomic status, gender and other differences.

It is important to remember that developing intercultural understanding is a lifelong process for all of us, and we are all continually developing our intercultural awareness, sensitivity, knowledge and skills.

PAUSE FOR REFLECTION

What are your assumptions about different ethnic groups?

How do you respond to difference?

What are your attitudes towards different languages?

How do you feel when you hear people speaking a different language?

The danger of a single story

Nigerian author, Chimamanda Ngozi Adiche, is a favourite writer of mine. In her powerful 2009 TED Talk, 'The Danger of a Single Story', she speaks about the danger of creating stereotypes when we only have a single story about other people and places. She recounts her personal experiences of having a single story, and of others who had a single story about her – such as her American roommate at university in the United States who was surprised she spoke English so well and thought she listened to 'tribal music' because she was African. She says, 'The single story creates stereotypes. And the problem with stereotypes is not that they are untrue, but that they are incomplete. They make one story become the only story.' She believes that it is necessary to engage with all of the stories of a person or place in order to engage properly. She says, 'The consequence of the single story is this: It robs people of dignity. It makes our recognition of our equal humanity difficult. It emphasises how we are different rather than how we are similar.' We can help our students to see that we are each unique and that our lives are made up of our many stories.

The greatest gift we can give children is to really see them, and to take the time to really know them and to see and honour their differences. It is the greatest gift we can give their families as well.

PAUSE FOR REFLECTION

We have all likely believed a single story at some time in our lives. I know I have and I now recognise the danger.

Consider a time when you believed a single story about another person, race or ethnic group. How did it affect your beliefs?

Consider a time you learned more than one story about another person, race, or ethnic group. How did it affect your beliefs? Did it change your perception?

What is needed to engage with the stories of a place or person?

Ourselves as lifelong learners

Our classrooms and schools are increasingly multicultural, multiracial and multilingual, and we are constantly learning alongside our students. Teaching and learning for intercultural understanding requires that we are active learners, who are both participating in the learning process and facilitating the learning process for our students at the same time. We cannot possibly know all there is to know about every different culture, but we can develop an awareness of difference and the willingness to find out and engage with others who are different from ourselves. We can continue our own lifelong learning about cultures, languages, history, geography, politics, economics, religions and beliefs that helps inform our teaching for intercultural understanding. I find that learning another language is very helpful in developing intercultural understanding and I encourage all teachers to do so. It improves communication with others, helps us to know another culture and promotes our own appreciation and respect for diversity.

The European Council of International Schools (ECIS) offered a year-long programme for international educators called the International Teachers Certificate (ITC), which was in place for many years up until 2017. It identified a set of attitudes and skills that internationally-minded 21st century teachers should possess. I have included them here as I believe they are foundational for developing intercultural understanding in ourselves, and that they are valuable for all teachers in all schools.

They are:

- a knowledge and appreciation of one's own culture and an openness to other cultures
- an openness to the points of view of people from different countries, cultures, religions and languages
- a willingness to learn other languages and an understanding of the cultural value of multilingualism
- an appreciation of the way that differences can enrich and enhance the teaching and learning of students of all ages
- an ability to incorporate into the teaching repertoire the values of cooperative learning and peaceful (or negotiated or non-violent) conflict resolution
- an inclusive approach that honours the experience and values of international students (*and I would say all students*) as a means of enriching the learning of the class as a whole
- the aim of ensuring that all students gain cross-cultural awareness and understanding as well as the skills to solve problems that inevitably arise in a globalised world
- a recognition of the importance of developing global citizens
- competency in using ICT in teaching and learning.

4

Exploring culture and language

Introduction

The concept of culture

The concept of culture is complex. Culture is dynamic and fluid, multifaceted and variable. Culture is a shared way of life that includes values, beliefs, attitudes, behaviours, languages and customs, and is passed on from one generation to the next. Culture is expressed through the clothes we wear, the food we eat, the languages we speak, the ways we behave, the artefacts we make and use, the traditions we follow and the festivals we celebrate. All of these aspects of culture reflect our underlying values and what is important to us. It is through our culture that we develop our perceptions of what is right or wrong, good or bad, polite or impolite, beautiful or ugly. Culture is the way we see the world and the way we live our lives.

I very much like the way Barrett et al. (2014) have explained the concept of culture as it helps us to understand its complexity. They acknowledge that culture is difficult to define because cultural groups are internally heterogeneous, and the individuals within them adhere to a range of diverse beliefs and practices. These beliefs and practices are also constantly changing and evolving over time. They suggest that culture consists of three aspects, *material, social* and *subjective*, each with its own resources. The material aspect includes resources that are used by the group such as tools, food and clothing. The social aspect includes the shared social institutions of the group such as language, religion and rules of social conduct. The subjective aspect refers to the values, attitudes, beliefs and practices, which group members use to make sense of and relate to the world.

They suggest that by defining culture in this way any social group has a distinct culture such as national, ethnic, faith, linguistic, generational, familial, school, etc. We all belong to multiple groups and therefore have many cultural influences that form our unique cultural identity. We use the resources available in each group and identify with each group to different degrees. Therefore we each have a unique cultural positioning that is formed by the intersection of the cultural groups we are affiliated with, our life histories, our personal experiences and individual personalities.

And while there are differences between cultures there are also differences within cultures. Each culture has subcultures, or groups within a group. For example, I live in Lucca, Italy, and within Italy there are cultural differences between regions such as Tuscany and Lazio, and within regions there are cultural differences between cities such as Lucca and Pisa, and within cities there are cultural differences between neighbourhoods. Cultural differences exist here in the city of Lucca if you live inside the city walls or outside the walls. We therefore cannot make assumptions about other people's culture – particularly based on nationality, race or ethnicity. While there are some cultural traits that may be shared we must get to know people to know their story and who they are.

Children first learn about culture from their families and the communities in which they live. The cultures we grow up in have a profound impact on our lives and shape the way we see the world. It is important to help children learn about, understand and take pride in their cultural heritage and learn about, understand and see the value and richness in the cultures of others. We can help children see the similarities, and accept and appreciate the differences that exist between cultures.

Explore the differences that exist in gestures, such as greeting someone. Do you kiss, bow or shake hands? In some cultures people kiss once on the cheek, yet in others it may be two or even three times. Others may hug or pat each other on the shoulder. Use of eye contact may also differ from culture to culture. In many cultures it is respectful to use direct eye contact when speaking with someone, while in others it is considered a sign of respect to avert one's eyes. There are many different ways of eating as well. Some people use a knife and fork, while others may use chopsticks or eat with their hands.

(Rader and Sittig, 2003)

Intercultural situations arise when we encounter someone who we perceive to have cultural affiliations that are different from our own. These can involve people from different national, regional, racial, linguistic, ethnic or faith backgrounds, or people who are different because of their lifestyle, socioeconomic status, age, etc. As we develop the disposition and competence of intercultural understanding we are better able to understand, and interact and communicate with others who are different from us.

'The important thing is to teach children to observe difference and foster an interest in learning how and why people do what they do.' Cultural differences can be regarded as strange or even threatening but with openness and understanding, we can accept them as simply a different way of doing things and being in the world. They can be fascinating and enriching.

(Rader and Sittig, 2003)

Iceberg Model of Culture

Cultural anthropologist, Edward T Hall, first used the iceberg as a model for culture. He suggested that the tip of the iceberg represented external or surface culture that was easily visible and that internal or deep culture was hidden below the surface.

I find the Iceberg Model of Culture a simple and effective model to use with children, and to help us all understand the different aspects of culture. The tip of the iceberg is visible above the water while the larger part lies below its surface. The aspects of culture that are most readily apparent such as food, clothing, language, festivals, traditions, art, dance and music are visible above the water line. However, the deeper aspects of culture such as our values, beliefs, thought processes and perceptions are invisible and lie below the surface. The image of the iceberg provides a clear visual model of how a large part of culture is not readily apparent or observable. This helps us to understand that there is much more to culture than we can see. The Iceberg Model of Culture can be used to illustrate the cultural aspects that are visible and invisible with any cultural group.

Many different iceberg models have been created and I suggest the one developed by John Penstone as it is comprehensive and clear:

http://opengecko.com/interculturalism/visualising-the-iceberg-model-of-culture

You could adapt The Culture Iceberg activity developed by the Peace Corps for use with children in Years 4–6 (www.peacecorps.gov/educators/resources/culture-iceberg), or simply choose to use the Penstone model to explain the concept that there are more aspects of culture that are hidden than are visible.

Dimensions of culture

In his book, *Beyond Culture* (1976), Hall describes some of the differences in culture that he observed and that are helpful to understand as we interact with diverse groups of people. In *high context* cultures individuals are less verbal and the listener must rely more on the context to understand what is being communicated. In *low context* cultures individuals are highly verbal, clear and to the point in their communication, and rely less on the context. Examples of high context cultures are Asian, Arab, Latino, African and African-American cultures and examples of low context cultures are Anglo-European American, Scandinavian and German cultures.

Hall also recognised differences in how people view and experience the concepts of time and space. Monochronic cultures tend to do one thing at a time and are quite punctual. Polychronic cultures tend to do many things at once and be more fluid in their use of time. Cultures also vary with proxemics, or the use of space, and differ in how people use personal space – such as how close people sit or stand to one another and how they view ownership of physical space. Cultural misunderstandings can occur when we do not understand these cultural differences, and judge or make assumptions about others.

Dutch social psychologist, Geert Hofstede, developed a framework for cross-cultural communication that is widely used in cross-cultural training in business. (Hofstede, 2001; Hofstede et al., 2010). Through his work with employees at IBM in the 1960s and 1970s he identified six dimensions of national culture that reflect cultural values, which can help us to understand the cultural differences we encounter in others. Different cultures fall somewhere on the continuum between low and high in each dimension. It is helpful to be aware of and understand these cultural differences, as they will likely arise with the children, parents and colleagues you work with.

The six dimensions of culture are:

Power Distance

Power Distance is the extent to which the less powerful members of society accept that power is distributed unequally. Some cultures are hierarchical and others strive to create a more equal sharing of power. This can be seen in the way children and parents respond to you as a teacher in a position of authority. For example, some parents or students may accept the decisions made by you or the school and others may question or challenge them. You may find that some parents and students establish more formal or informal relationships with you.

Individualist vs. Collectivist

In Individualist cultures people are expected to take care of only themselves and their immediate family. In Collectivist cultures people expect the in-groups they belong to, such as families or organisations, to look after them in exchange for loyalty. You may find that some children may not speak up unless asked by you or their classmates to do so and are more comfortable with group presentations, while others take the initiative and are equally comfortable with presenting on their own.

Masculinity vs. Femininity

Masculinity refers to an emphasis on status, achievement and success in life, and society is generally more competitive. Femininity refers to an emphasis on the quality of life, serving others and cooperation, and society is more consensus-building. These are not gender stereotypes but suggest what is highly valued in a society and can be true for any gender.

Uncertainty Avoidance

Uncertainty Avoidance refers to the extent to which people feel threatened by uncertainty and ambiguity, and try to avoid such situations. You may see this in some children who need to know the right answer and others who are more comfortable with more open-ended tasks.

Long-Term Orientation

Long-Term Orientation is the extent to which a society exhibits a pragmatic future-oriented perspective rather than a conventional historical or short-term point of view.

Indulgence and Restraint

Indulgence refers to the free gratification of desires while Restraint refers to suppressed gratification that is governed by social norms. In some cultures people like and expect an immediate response or reward, and in others they expect to wait for a period of time.

The Hofstede Insights and Geert Hofstede websites describe the six dimensions of national culture more thoroughly and include comparisons of culture from different countries.
See: www.hofstede-insights.com or https://geert-hofstede.com
Cultural differences may explain the reasons your students are hesitant to participate in class, or may not arrive to school on time or make direct eye contact. It is important to consider that cultural differences may be the underlying reason behind certain attitudes and behaviours. It is helpful to observe the differences you see, become knowledgeable about cultural differences, and utilise students, parents, caregivers and colleagues as cultural resources to help learn about and understand cultural differences. When we help children learn about how different people and families live and communicate, we both welcome them into the classroom and prepare them to thrive as intercultural learners.

PAUSE FOR REFLECTION

As you reflect on the work of Hall and Hofstede consider the following questions:

What are some of the cultural differences you have observed in the children in your classroom?

What are some of the cultural differences you have observed in the parents or caregivers of your students?

What are some of the cultural differences you have observed in your colleagues?

Culture and language are inextricably linked

Language is an integral part of culture. It is through language that culture and its knowledge, traditions and shared values are conveyed, understood, expressed and preserved. Byram (1997), cited in Williams-Gualandi (2015), recognises that language and culture are linked and that 'the acquisition of foreign language is the acquisition of the cultural practices and beliefs it embodies for particular social groups'.
The linguistic diversity in our world reflects the cultural diversity that exists, and the languages we speak are an essential part of our cultural identity. The United Nations Convention on the

Post-reading activities

- Based on the book add to the chart you started about what you know about Japanese culture.
- Chart the similarities and differences the children learned between Japanese and American culture. Make sure to point out that while some customs were clearly different, both children's families did some things in both Western and Japanese ways, and people often adopt some aspects of different cultures into their own.

    The illustrations are quite rich and tell us a lot about Japanese culture. Draw on these and the text for the following activities.

- Just as the children in this book learned about each other's cultures and languages your students can learn about each other's cultures and languages, too. Create a class book entitled (*Melbourne, Berlin, Beijing* or wherever you are) *Friends*. Based on *Tokyo Friends* create a page for each of the different customs, in the cultures and languages of your class.

    You could include:

    ways to say hello

    ways to greet each other

    a traditional breakfast

    how books and text are read (for example Arabic, Hebrew and Chinese are read right to left)

    a traditional lunch from their culture

    how you count, read numbers or do maths (for example, in German numbers are read right to left such as 21 as *einundzwansig*

    polite manners when eating a traditional dinner, or eating in a traditional restaurant

    ways to bathe and keep clean

    others you and your students choose!

- The author takes us through the calendar year telling us about the following Japanese festivals, celebrations or events that happen each month. Have your students work in small groups to research and teach their classmates about some of the following or others they find of interest:

    January – Japanese New Year

    February – Setsubun (Japanese Bean Throwing Festival before the first day of spring – 3rd or 4th Feb)

    March – Hinamatsuri (Girls' Day) 3rd March

    April – Cherry Blossom Festival

    May – Kodomo no hi (Children's Day) 5th May

    June – Boating in Inokashira Park

    July – Tanabata (Star Festival) 7th July

    August – Aomori Nebuta Matsuri 2nd to 7th August; Obon: Festival of the Dead

    September – Sumo wrestling tournament

    October – Halloween parade in Omotesandō, the main shopping street in Tokyo

    November – Shichi-Go-San (Celebrating 3–5–7 year-olds) 15th November

    December – Year-end gift giving.

They could also research the Zen Buddhist temples, including the Great Buddha, and Shinto shrines in Kamakura.

Look for similarities and differences between cultures such as the Obon Festival in Japan and the Day of the Dead in Mexico.

- Explore the experience of sharing cultures with others. Give the children a sheet of paper and ask them to fold it in half. On one side have the children write and draw about something they learned about another culture from someone else. On the other side have them write and draw about something they taught someone else about their culture. Have each child share his or her examples, and tell what they liked about both learning from and teaching others.

- Explain to your students that manners and etiquette differ between cultures and can be tricky. We learned that it is considered polite to slurp when eating noodles in Japan but not in American culture. Have your students research the differences between cultures in polite and impolite behaviours such as spitting, slurping, making eye contact, giving flowers, sticking out your tongue, cleaning your plate, etc. Invite them to share any personal experiences.

- Katie, Keiko and Kenji learned about each other's cultures and languages from each other. How can we learn about different cultures and languages from our classmates? Your students will have many ideas such as learning useful phrases, vocabulary and numbers in their languages, cooking typical foods, or learning games, songs and dances from their cultures.

- This book was written in 1998. While many traditions are still the same, some may have changed. Explore the ways culture changes over time and compare aspects of Japanese culture today with the past.

Suggested follow-up activities

- Learn more about Japan and Japanese culture. Invite parents, colleagues or members of the community to teach the children Japanese calligraphy, watercolour painting or *ikebana*, the Japanese art of flower arranging or *bonsai*, a Japanese tea ceremony, or about Manga, Japanese comics.

- The second part of the book highlights Japanese celebrations, festivals and events throughout the year. Have each child create a book about the celebrations, festivals and events they celebrate with their families each month throughout the year. Have the children write and draw, and label their illustrations in their home languages as well as English. Alternatively, you could create a class Big Book.

- Have your students research the Buddhist and Shinto religions, and the faith-based and secular beliefs such as Humanism in your class. Some of your students may have multi-faith backgrounds. Include any languages that are used in particular religions. Invite families to share their celebrations and why they are meaningful with the class.

Links with learning outcomes in other chapters

This book links with learning outcomes in the following chapters:

Chapter 5: 'Understanding and valuing personal and cultural identity'

Learners will:
Understand how our identity is shaped and can change.

- Keiko is an American growing up in Japan. As she adopts some of the Japanese customs she is learning she may begin to feel both American and Japanese. She may be influenced by her Japanese friends, others she and her family have met, and living in the new culture. Ask if

Post-reading activities

- Have the children turn and talk to a neighbour and share a wishing tradition that was new to them or that they found most interesting and why. Have several children share with the whole class.

- Have the children create their own *Wish* books that tell about the wishing traditions in their families. Include home languages where appropriate. This could also be a lovely project to do with a buddy from another year group.

- Have the children share any wishing traditions from other countries, cultures or religions that they have adopted and added to their lives.

- Invite other members of the school community to share their wishing traditions with the children. This could include specialist and other classroom teachers, administrators, bus drivers, maintenance staff and others.

- The author's endnotes give interesting background information about each of the wishing traditions included in the book, and help the children learn how beliefs and practices have been influenced by other cultures who have brought their traditions with them when they moved to new places. I suggest you take the time to read these, too.

- On the last page of the book the illustrator has drawn lucky symbols. The children could include lucky symbols from their cultures or religions in their wish books and/or bring in cultural artefacts that are considered lucky to them.

Suggested follow-up activities

- Learn about other cultural, religious and family traditions in addition to wishing. Have each child create a book about the traditions in his or her family to include other traditions and rituals such as birthdays, weddings, the birth of a new baby, the death of a loved one, naming ceremonies and others. This can be done with children of all ages, and parents or caregivers can help young children decide which traditions and rituals they would like to include. Have the children share their books in a class presentation, with other classes, cross-year buddies and parents.

- Celebrate the wishing traditions of the children in your class throughout the year. Make a short video clip of each celebration, and compile in a video of wishing traditions of the class to share with others.

- Have your students collect photographs of wishing traditions from around the world and create a photography exhibition for the school. Alternatively, they could ask children and adults in the school community to submit photographs of the wishing traditions in their families, and create a school-wide display of wishing traditions.

Links with learning outcomes in other chapters

Chapter 6: Cultivating Transformative Beliefs, Values and Attitudes

The learning engagements in this lesson plan also meet these learning outcomes:

Learners will:
Develop genuine curiosity about and interest in other people, their cultures and lives.
Develop enjoyment and appreciation of different cultural experiences.

5

Understanding and valuing personal and cultural identity

Introduction

In *New Kid in School: Using Literature to Help Children in Transition* (Rader and Sittig, 2003) I developed the concept of transition education where children are intentionally taught about the experience of moving, nationally or internationally, and develop knowledge, skills and attitudes to help them thrive in the new school environment. At the heart of transition education is affirming and celebrating children's unique backgrounds and experiences, which includes valuing their cultures, languages and identity, and developing self-awareness.

Personal and cultural identity is one of the six components of my Model of Transition Education (1998) (see Rader and Sittig, 2003, p. 4). Chapter 4, 'Personal and cultural identity', addresses our identity as an integral part of transition education, and highlights its value. A strong transition education programme also develops intercultural understanding and international-mindedness in children, and I draw on this work here.

What personal and cultural identity is, and its importance

What is it that makes us uniquely who we are?

Each one of us is unique. Our identity, or sense of self, is formed by our own individual combination of cultures, languages, personal traits, temperament, interests, preferences and life experiences. It is both personal and cultural. While our personal and cultural identities are inextricably linked, the culture or cultures we grow up in significantly influence our identity, and help shape the way we see and experience the world.

We are often unaware of the ways that our cultures shape our identity, as our culture learning is largely unconscious. However, our identity is the essence of who we are, and we benefit in all areas of our lives from understanding ourselves and others more deeply. Our personal and cultural identities influence all of the roles we may have in life such as who we are as teachers, colleagues, parents, partners, neighbours and friends. In our schools we bring our cultures, languages, life experiences and passions to our work with children, their families and our colleagues.

It is through understanding and valuing our own personal and cultural identity that we are able to recognise the value that personal and cultural identity holds for others as well. As we come to understand its importance to ourselves we also understand its importance to others. This is a necessary beginning for developing intercultural understanding and regard for others.

Our personal and cultural identity is both constant and fluid.

There are aspects of our cultures, and personal traits and preferences that remain a constant part of our identity throughout our lives. Others may change over time depending on the groups we identify with and participate in, our relationships and the life experiences we have. Our personal and cultural identity continues to evolve throughout our lives.

Our personal and cultural identity may not coincide with our national identity or the identity of other family members.

Children's cultural identity may or may not coincide with their national identity or the identity of other family members if they have grown up outside of their passport country: for example a British child living in Japan may identify more strongly with the Japanese culture than the British one. Even when the child moves away from Japan he or she may always identify with some aspects of Japanese culture. If siblings have grown up in different countries or cultures they may have a different identity as well.

(Rader and Sittig, 2003)

Understanding and valuing our personal and cultural identity leads to greater self-esteem and self-confidence.

As we are increasingly aware of our identity, we come to know ourselves more deeply and can engage in all of life with a greater sense of competence. It gives us grounding and contributes to healthy self-esteem and self-confidence, and the belief that we can manage whatever changes and challenges we may face.

We can retain our personal and cultural identity and also integrate into new cultures, contexts and communities.

With self-awareness and confidence we can integrate into new cultural and social situations and also stay true to our personal and cultural identity. Educators and parents can support children in this endeavour and help them see the benefit of both.

Learning outcomes

Learners will:

- Begin to understand what personal and cultural identity is, and its importance for themselves and others.
- Gain an awareness of their growing and developing personal and cultural identity.
- Understand how our identity is shaped and can change.
- Develop greater self-esteem and self-confidence.
- Recognise the cultural influences in their lives that help make them who they are.
- Gain a greater understanding of the personal and cultural identity of others (their classmates, teachers, family, neighbours).
- Understand the difference between 'fitting in' and 'belonging'.

References

Brown, B (2012) *Daring Greatly: How the Courage to be Vulnerable Transforms the Way We Live, Love, Parent and Lead*. New York, NY: Avery.

Pollock, D and Van Reken, R (2009) *Third Culture Kids: Growing Up Among Worlds*. Boston, MA: Nicholas Brealey Publishing.

Rader, D and Sittig, L (2003) *New Kid in School: Using Literature to Help Children in Transition*. New York, NY: Teachers College Press.

Selasi, T (2014) 'Don't Ask Where I'm From, Ask Where I'm a Local'. TED Talk October 2014. www.ted.com/talks/taiye_selasi_don_t_ask_where_i_m_from_ask_where_i_m_a_local

Develop tolerance and respect for others and their differences.

Develop an enjoyment and appreciation of different cultural experiences, and begin to seek them out.

This story provides an opportunity to develop empathy and compassion for children who are new, and explore ways to welcome new students from different cultures and who speak a different language. Children can develop a greater appreciation and respect for diversity, and curiosity and interest in learning about other cultures and languages through examining Joey and Unhei's characters.

- Why do you think the children on the bus made fun of Unhei's name? Following the children's responses, explain that sometimes people laugh when words or names sound different. Why is that? Possible answers might be they may feel embarrassed, think it's funny, and they do not think about how their words or actions might affect the other person.

- Lead a discussion about the impact our words and actions can have, both positive and negative. Explain that our words and actions are powerful, and we do not always think about the effect they have on others. Examine the text for examples of words or actions that were hurtful or embarrassing to Unhei. These include the children chanting and making fun of her name on the bus, the girl who scrunched up her face when she heard Unhei's name, even Joey who was trying to be helpful announced loudly, 'Here's the new girl!' when she entered the classroom, and a boy making a joke that maybe she robbed a bank in Korea and needs a new identity.

  Have the children identify other situations where people might scrunch up their face when faced with difference such as different food, clothing, language, accent, hairstyle, music, etc. and how that might make the person feel. What message does it give?

- What are other ways they could have responded? Possible answers are they could have shown interest in Unhei and her culture, asked her where she was from, introduced themselves, tried to pronounce her name and asked for help pronouncing it. This is an excellent opportunity to discuss why no one on the bus spoke out when the others teased Unhei, and what they could have said or done. Continue the conversation to explore the difference between being a bystander, an upstander or change-maker, and what we can do to move from silence and inaction to taking action.

- What words and actions had a positive impact? The children were kind and tried to help her find a new name. Joey reached out to her. Chart both of these to make the learning visible.

- The other children in Unhei's class were trying to be kind and helpful by providing a Name Jar for her. How could they have been kind and helpful in a way that honoured Unhei's language and culture? Ideas could include: prepared for her arrival by learning greetings in Korean, created a bilingual phrasebook with useful phrases including inclusive questions such as 'Do you want to play?', showed an interest in her name and asked her to help them learn to pronounce it correctly, showed an interest in learning Korean and helped her learn more words and phrases in English.

- I think it is a worthy discussion to examine the character of Mr Cocotos, the class teacher. Tell your students you are curious about Mr Cocotos. Ask them what they notice about him. He did not seem to know Unhei's name when he introduced her to the class. He allowed the Name Jar and also seemed concerned when it went missing. Explain that children and adults can learn from each other. Have your students write a letter/email to Mr Cocotos suggesting ways the class could plan to welcome Unhei before she arrives. Consider ways they could learn more about each other before her first day, including the use of social media.

- In small groups have the students discuss, 'How could we welcome new students who speak another language, and are moving from another country and culture?'. Move around the room and listen in to the conversations, extending the children's thinking. Invite each group to share a suggestion with the whole class. Chart their responses and strategies. Include them in a class Welcome Manual or Welcome Video, and invite student choice for further ideas. What could you and your classmates do to welcome new students and honour their cultures and languages? How could you make them feel like they belong and are part of the class?

- Joey has many qualities that demonstrate intercultural understanding. Explain that Joey is an important character in this story. Have your students work in groups of three to discuss Joey's character traits. How would you describe him? Give examples. Possible answers might include friendly, kind, curious, interested in other cultures, a leader, takes the initiative, is a problem-solver, independent thinker, etc. Have each group complete a Character/Trait/Evidence chart. You could do the same for Unhei (see below).

- How did Joey show kindness and friendship to Unhei? (He pulled her into the classroom and introduced her to the class, he introduced himself and asked what her real name was, he was curious and interested in her culture, and appreciated its beauty, he sought out a Korean name for himself, he took the Name Jar and encouraged Unhei to keep her Korean name.)

- How would you describe Unhei? What qualities did she have? Possible answers may be she was patient, gracious and appreciative of the 'funny and beautiful names' the children chose for her, friendly, brave, kind and open-minded. Explore ways she was brave. She corrected the kids on the bus and spelled her name, smiled when she entered the class even though she was scared, said she didn't have a name to give herself time to consider the problem, and chose her own name in the end, even if the other kids wanted her to choose one of the names they suggested.

Joey learned about how names are chosen in Korea and how a name stamp is used as a person's signature. He took the initiative to go to the Korean shop and have a name stamp made for himself so he could sign his name in Korean, too. Ask your students to reflect on ways they have incorporated aspects of another culture into their own lives. Examples might be instruments they play, music they listen to, recipes they prepare or mindfulness practice. Share your personal examples if appropriate.

Chapter 7: 'Engaging with difference'

Learners will:
Seek commonalities and learn about 'reaching in' and 'reaching out'.
Explore the emotions associated with change, discomfort and uncertainty, and healthy ways to address them.
Engage with others who are different from themselves and begin to develop multicultural relationships.

- Joey reaches out to Unhei from the start and begins to develop a friendship with her. Explain that for relationships to grow and develop we need to respond when others reach out to us. Joey took the initiative and reached out to Unhei by asking about her name and showing interest in it and in her. She responded by showing him her name stamp and offering him the chance to try it. In fact that may have inspired him to get one of his own. She shared her umbrella as they walked to the bus together. Both 'reaching out' and responding are necessary for friendships to develop. Ask, How have you reached out to others who were new? Others who are different from you? Other kids you met on holiday or in a new group you joined? How could you reach out to others in new situations? Share your own personal examples if relevant.

- Collect all of the stories, both children's and adults', and publish them in a class book for your class library. Create a guide for 'reaching in' and 'reaching out' that could be shared online with other children around the world.

- Consider having your students write to answer the following questions in a Reflection Journal, Learning Log or on a class blog: How have you responded when others have reached out to you? Do you shy away or engage with them? Why or why not? Have you ever reached out to someone who is new or different from you? How did you feel in each situation? How did you react? What qualities helped you or hindered you? What might you do next time?

Explain that 'reaching in' is equally important when people arrive in a new community. How could Unhei have 'reached in' to the new culture in which she is now living? She could have asked Joey or the other kids to teach her about life in America. What games or sports are popular? Are there certain foods that people like? What do people do to relax or have fun?

Have you ever 'reached in' to a new group or place? How did you do it? How could you have 'reached in'?

What have you learned from your friends from different cultures, and what have they learned from you?

Can you give an example(s) of when you have sought out different cultural experiences on your own or with your family? What captured your interest? What did you learn? What are you interested in learning more about?

What have you learned from Unhei and Joey?

Chapter 8: 'Developing essential intercultural, interpersonal and life skills'

Learners will:
Develop greater intercultural awareness and sensitivity.
Develop increased problem-solving and decision-making skills.

- The children will develop greater intercultural awareness and sensitivity as they learn about the origins of each other's names, and recognise how important they are to their classmates.

- Discuss the way Unhei's class developed greater sensitivity to her cultural background.

At the end of the story Unhei explains that she decided to choose her own name because Korean names mean something and she liked it best. Mr Cocotos mentioned that many American names have meanings, too. They all applauded Unhei's choice and practised pronouncing her name correctly, including Mr Cocotos.

- Discuss the way Unhei arrived at her decision to keep her Korean name. What was her process? What did she do? Possible answers might be she explored the options by trying out the American names in the Name Jar at home, she reflected on what was important to her such as her family, her culture, her mother's opinion, her grandmother's gift and Joey's encouragement. Have your students draw and/or write about their decision-making process.

Personal notes

I used this book with third grade children at an international school in Italy with great success. As the children shared their stories they were clearly proud of their names and family stories of how and why they were chosen, and they were keenly interested in the stories of their classmates. The stories were personal and absolutely beautiful.

Here are a few examples:

'My name is Diyora. My parents named me in memory of my great grandmother. My name comes from the Tartar language and means 'beloved'. My parents really liked the name, also because it sounded beautiful.'

'My name is Salman. My grandmother selected my name. My name means 'peace'. It is a traditional Arabic name. The root meaning of my name is 'safe'. Be safe, secure, at peace and be healthy.'

'My name is Beatrice. My parents thought it was a sweet, romantic and timeless name. It comes from Latin and it means 'the lady that makes you happy'. My parents chose my name when I was in my mum's tummy. She usually spoke with me and she was sure of my name. She was sure that a unique joy was coming in her life.'

As I read *The Name Jar* to the children I could see the growing concern on their faces as Unhei read out the names, thinking that she might choose another name and not her own. There was a collective sigh of relief when she chose her Korean name in the end and in fact, it was met with applause by some!

Following this lesson the Grade 3 class teacher compiled the children's stories behind their names in a class book, which she said remained a favourite in their class library for the rest of the school year. There are many ways it can be published and shared, either digitally or as a hard copy.

Lesson plan: Reception–Year 6

Personal and cultural identity map project
Based on My Map Book *by Sara Fanelli*
Create a map of your personal and cultural self!

Synopsis

I have long-loved *My Map Book* by Sara Fanelli and have used it often as an introduction to map work and a variety of map projects with children. It is a charming and whimsical book of vibrant, brightly-coloured maps that reflect the author's inner and outer world as a child. In addition to more common maps such as a 'Map of My Neighborhood' and a 'Map of My Bedroom', she includes creative maps such as a 'Map of My Family', a 'Map of My Dog' and a 'Map of My Heart', which delight children of all ages – and adults, too! Sara's imaginative concepts and drawings inspire our own creativity and help us see maps in a whole new way. This book provides an excellent way to introduce the personal and cultural identity map project.

Learning outcomes

Learners will:

- Begin to understand what personal and cultural identity is, and its importance for themselves and others.
- Gain an awareness of their growing and developing personal and cultural identity.
- Begin to understand that their identity is shaped by their families, cultures and life experiences, and can change as they grow up.
- Develop greater self-esteem and self-confidence.
- Identify the cultural influences from the people, places and beliefs in their lives that help make them who they are (★Years 3–6).
- Gain a greater understanding of the personal and cultural identity of their classmates, teachers, family and neighbours.

Planning the project

I have found this project to be a powerful and meaningful learning experience, and it is one that you will likely refer back to during the school year. ★Please see the 'Notes for Reception–Year 2' at the end of this plan.

This project has been planned for three sessions, however, it can be adapted to fit your schedule. During the first session share the book, have your students complete an identity chart and plan the project (see templates in Appendix H). In the second session the children create the actual map. Allow adequate time between these two sessions for thinking through ideas, planning and gathering materials. In the third session your students write or dictate a description of their personal and cultural identity as is reflected on their map. This project can be easily adapted for younger children through the language you use and the examples you share.

Create your own Personal and Cultural Identity Map to share with your students. They will appreciate knowing more about you, and in turn they will be willing to share who they are more deeply. And it is fun!

Session one

Pre-reading activities

- Introduce the project by explaining to your students that today we will begin a special map project. Initiate a discussion about the nature of maps. What is a map? What different kinds of maps are there? Why do we use maps? Establish that a map is a picture or drawing of a place, and its features or characteristics. Have the children name some of the different kinds of maps there are such as city, state, country, world, road, museum, school, park, tourist, etc.

- Name some of the uses of maps such as to locate places, find out how to get places, learn more about a place, and help us explore and make sense of the world around us. Have examples of maps you can show the class, and include maps that are pertinent to the place you all currently live such as a Tube map, A–Z or map of London Zoo if you live in London. With young children you might have a treasure map or map of the classroom to share.

- Gather your students up close so they can see the book well. Introduce *My Map Book* by Sara Fanelli saying that Sara has created a unique collection of maps. They are personal maps about her when she was a child. Ask the children to think about what we can learn about Sara from her maps. Invite the children to ask questions, share observations and connections, or comment on something they like about each map as you read the book.

Post-reading activities

- Discuss: When Sara made her maps she included people and things she loves and that are important to her. Have the children share what they learned about Sara from her maps. Possible answers might be she loves books, her family, her dog Bubu, spaghetti, cakes and chocolate, the moon, maps, she shares a room with her sister, has story time before bed, has a good imagination, etc.

- Introduce the Personal and Cultural Identity Map project. Tell your students that they, too, are going to create a different kind of map; a map that tells about who they are so that we can learn more about ourselves and each other, just like we learned about Sara. They will a create map of their personal and cultural selves, a Personal and Cultural Identity Map. You might call it a 'Map of Me!' or similar with younger children.

- Explain that each one of us is unique and special, and has our own identity. Discuss the meaning of identity. Establish that our identity is our sense of who we are and how we see ourselves. It's what makes you, you and me, me. It is your own individual combination of cultures, languages, personal traits, life experiences, values, passions, interests and preferences. Our personal identity and our cultural identity are closely linked together to make us who we are.

- Ask what kinds of things could you include on your map that tell about your personal and cultural self. Together generate a list of ideas and give an example of each.

Ideas may include: people, places and things we love such as family and pets; the languages we speak; the places we are from and have lived; our favourite hobbies and activities; our passions and interests; our faiths or beliefs; family traditions; what is important to us; festivals and celebrations;

- Explain that you will begin reading a novel that helps us understand the value and importance of our personal and cultural identity. You could introduce the idea of keeping a reading response journal during the reading of this book for your students to sketch and/or write about their thoughts, observations, questions and connections. They could use these reflections and notes to create a final book project about an aspect of the story that was most meaningful to them.

Post-reading activities

- Discuss Margie's identity at the beginning of the story, how it changed and why. How did her self-esteem and self-confidence change?
- On page 2 Margie mentions that Lupe was not as lucky as she was to be born in the United States. It is an important point to discuss that children do not choose where and when they are born, and are deserving of respect and caring regardless of their situation.
- Discuss the difference between 'fitting in' and 'belonging'. What did Margie do to 'fit in' to American culture? Possible answers are she chose not to learn and speak Spanish, she changed her name, curled her hair, rejected her cousin, Lupe, and her Mexican heritage. What was the impact? What do you think it was like for Margie to keep up the image that she was American? What did she learn?
- Re-read pages 132–33. Margie learns that she can appreciate and value both her Mexican and American heritage. Have your students write about what they appreciate and value about their cultural heritage.
- At the end of the story (page 134) Margarita (Margie) writes a beautiful essay entitled 'My Family', where she tells her story about her identity, and realises that she is both Mexican and American. Have your students write a letter to Margarita in response. What would they say to her? Have your students write an essay about their own families and identities, and share them with the class. Alternatively, they could create a Family History project.

Suggested follow-up activities

- The dress Margie's aunt made for her reflected her identity as a Mexican and an American. Have the children create multicultural self-portraits including clothing and accessories that reflect their multicultural backgrounds.
- Introduce the project 'I See You! I Know You!' (see below). Through this project the children learn about and depict the personal and cultural identity of a classmate.

  Together as a class develop a list of possible questions to ask to learn more about the other person's personal and cultural identity, such as what celebrations, languages spoken, nationalities, traditions, beliefs, values, interests and passions are important to the person, and are part of his or her life. Have the students work in pairs and interview each other to gather this information. Then have each student plan an art project to represent his or her partner's identity. This might be a mural, painting, sculpture, model, diorama, mobile, etc. Once the plan is complete have each student confer with his or her partner to make sure he or she has understood the person accurately, and to correct any misunderstandings if necessary. This is an integral part of the project and helps children develop stronger communication skills as they ask questions, listen well, clarify their understanding, and explain differences or misunderstandings respectfully.

  Have the students create the project at home or school. Have them introduce their partner and describe his or her identity through their project. Create an art gallery and plan a gallery walk so the children can learn more about the personal and cultural identities of their classmates.

Links with learning outcomes in other chapters

This book links with learning outcomes in the following chapters:

Chapter 4: 'Exploring culture and language'

Learners will:
Gain knowledge and appreciation of their own cultures and languages, and those of others, and develop an interest in learning about them.
Gain an understanding of how culture and language are connected.
Gain knowledge of different cultural beliefs including secular and faith-based practices.
Begin to understand the value of cultural and linguistic diversity.
Become knowledgeable about the similarities and differences between cultures.
Begin to understand the importance of developing and maintaining home languages.
Develop greater appreciation and respect for cultural and linguistic diversity.

This book provides excellent opportunities to discuss the importance of languages.

- Margie tells the principal Lupe cannot be in her class because she doesn't speak. The principal corrects her and says that Lupe doesn't speak English but she speaks Spanish. Discuss the reason this is an important point and help your students recognise that people have knowledge and skills in their own language, and all languages have value.

- Have your students learn about the value and importance of developing and maintaining home languages. Plan ways home languages can be celebrated and integrated throughout the school year and not only on International Mother Language Day.

- Discuss how research has changed people's attitudes and beliefs about English-only programmes. We now know that there are great advantages to being bilingual and multilingual. Have your students research the benefits of bilingualism and multilingualism, and the practice of translanguaging. Plan ways to share their findings with the school community and other schools worldwide. Choose ways to teach others in the school about translanguaging and the benefits of speaking other languages.

- In Chapter 18 Margie's family has a conversation where they alternate between Spanish and English. Explain that this is called code-switching and is a natural process for people who speak or are learning another language. They are using the knowledge and skills they have in their languages to communicate. Invite your students to share the examples of when they use code-switching when they communicate. Recognise how this practice is used in your classroom along with translanguaging.

- Margie is jealous of her mother's relationship with Lupe. Why do you think she feels this way? (They have an intimacy through speaking Spanish and sharing their Mexican culture.) What was Margie missing by not embracing her cultural heritage?

  She often feels left out of family conversations at home, and does not fully understand stories and humour because she does not speak Spanish. Discuss how language and culture are connected, and there are certain things that can only be expressed in the language of the culture. Discuss the advantages of being bilingual or multilingual. Discuss your students' feelings about learning another language.

6

Cultivating transformative beliefs, values and attitudes

Introduction

Beliefs, values and attitudes: a shared understanding of what they are

Our beliefs, values and attitudes are integral to living our lives with intercultural understanding. As we explore some of the *beliefs, values* and *attitudes* particularly relevant to intercultural understanding it is helpful to have a shared understanding of what we mean by these terms. I suggest the following definitions for the purpose of this book:

A *belief* is a conviction or opinion that something is true. It can also be a religious tenet or conviction. While our religious or spiritual beliefs may influence our beliefs in general, in this chapter I am referring to beliefs in a secular sense. For example, the belief that all languages and cultures have equal value or that cultural diversity enriches our world.

A *value* is something we hold as important in life. For example, the value of love, peace, freedom or education.

An *attitude* is a disposition or orientation towards a person or thing, a way of thinking or feeling about something. For example, open-mindedness towards other cultures, empathy, or appreciation and respect for diversity and difference.

However, our beliefs, values and attitudes are intertwined and cannot always be clearly defined as one or the other. They influence each other and often overlap. I shall therefore discuss them together as related concepts.

Our beliefs, values and attitudes can transform our lives and our world for good

We each develop our beliefs, values and attitudes from our families, cultural backgrounds, religious or spiritual practices, and life experiences. They are an intrinsic and important part of who we are and directly affect the way we live our lives. The beliefs, values and attitudes we hold directly influence our thoughts and feelings, and consequently our behaviour and the ways we interact and engage with others. They can move us to positive or negative action, or be the cause of indifference and inaction.

Cultivating beliefs, values and attitudes that honour and respect all others, infuse our lives with kindness and compassion, and preserve human dignity, human rights, and the health of our planet, has the power to transform our world for good.

As with all aspects of intercultural understanding, transformative beliefs, values and attitudes are developed throughout our lives. They can change as we develop greater knowledge and understanding, and we begin to live our lives aligned with the positive beliefs, values and attitudes we are learning. However, they cannot be left to chance but need to be developed intentionally, and modelled, practised and reinforced.

Paul Tough, author of *How Children Succeed: Grit, Curiosity and the Hidden Power of Character* (2012), asserts that, character traits do not just happen magically but are rooted in our brain chemistry and are molded by the environment in which children grow up. He argues that we are missing a fundamental part of being human when we focus solely on academics and do not attend to the character traits that are as important to develop.

We as educators must partner with families and caregivers, and communities to reinforce in children the positive beliefs, values and attitudes that may or may not be instilled at home, and to counter harmful ones. In constructing its framework to help shape what children learn for 2030 the OECD has created four propositions that are integral to the 2030 Framework. The second proposition states, 'The skills, attitudes and values that shape human behaviour should be rethought, to counter the discriminatory behaviours picked up at school and in the family' (OECD, 2015).

PAUSE FOR REFLECTION

What are the beliefs, values and attitudes you think are key to developing intercultural understanding?

What are the benefits of intentionally developing them?

What are the risks of not developing them?

The teaching of values in schools

Over the past few decades we have seen a renewed focus on the importance of teaching values and developing strong character in children. Given the particularly challenging times we are currently living in we are seeing a re-emergence of character education in schools around the world. Educators, world leaders and business leaders recognise the need to intentionally teach children the values and attitudes that are essential for living and working together in a globalised world, and to ensure peace, equity and sustainability.

Character education

Character education has always existed in some form in educational systems around the world. Its aim has been to develop ethical and moral purpose in children and good citizenship. We have seen its increase and decrease over the past decades for a variety of reasons such as a prevailing spirit of individualism beginning in the 1960s, doubt of its effectiveness or appropriateness in schools and competing priorities. With an increased focus on assessment and technology as well, character education became less prominent in schools.

However, with the current increased focus on consumerism and materialism, individual achievement and personal happiness, and growing racism and xenophobia, educators have seen the need to re-introduce character education in schools. Character education advocates intentionally developing universally acknowledged values and virtues for the good of all. 'The goal of character education is the good life: one in which we can flourish as human beings, achieve our potential and live meaningfully and harmoniously in communities with others' (University of Birmingham Jubilee Centre). Schools recognise the need to integrate character education into the curriculum and have found this creates healthy school communities and contributes to children's academic achievement, and social and emotional well-being.

In *The Road to Character*, David Brooks (2015) writes about the BIG ME culture where individuals who are self-promoting are rewarded and most likely to succeed. Brooks questions what this drive for wealth and status says about us as a human race, and suggests that it is virtues of character that give meaning to our lives.

We see evidence of character education in many forms. In IB schools the IB Learner Profile and Attitudes guide the development of beliefs, values and attitudes for international-mindedness. The Jubilee Centre for Character and Virtues at the University of Birmingham has created a *Framework for Character Education in Schools* and resources to support character development in the UK and beyond. The University of Birmingham is the first university to offer an MA in Character Education. You may wish to visit its website, www.jubileecentre.ac.uk.

Many schools in the UK and British schools around the world have integrated Values-based Education (VbE) into their curriculums.

Values-based Education is an approach to teaching that works with values. It creates a strong learning environment that enhances academic attainment, and develops students' social and relationship skills that last throughout their lives. VbE is an approach that nourishes, and enables learners to flourish, making a difference to the world through who and how they are.

(VbE website)

Schools worldwide are also incorporating The Virtues Project. 'The Virtues Project was founded in Canada in 1991 by Linda Kavelin-Popov, Dr Dan Popov and John Kavelin. It was honored by the United Nations during the International Year of the Family in 1994 as a 'model global program for families of all cultures'.

'The mission of The Virtues Project is to inspire people of all cultures to remember who we really are and to live by our highest values.' The Virtues Project is based on the idea, 'that all children are born with the virtues in potential, and that when parents and educators awaken these gifts of character, we can change the world.' The language of the virtues is affirming rather than shaming. For example, rather than call a child stubborn we could call on their cooperation or respect. 'Virtues are the content of our character, the elements of the human spirit. They grow stronger whenever we use them' (Virtues Project website).

As educators we can activate and strengthen the virtues in our work with children when we explicitly teach them, and encourage and reinforce their practice.

While all of the virtues identified lead to a fulfilling life, I believe the following particularly lend themselves to developing intercultural understanding: caring, compassion, confidence, courage, creativity, flexibility, honesty, humility, justice, kindness, peacefulness, respect, responsibility, tolerance and trustworthiness. These are reflected in my *Framework for Developing Intercultural Understanding* (Rader, 2016).

Geoff Smith is a Cornish Primary head teacher, whose successful integration of The Virtues Project at Kehelland Village School led to a commission from Birmingham University to produce the UK's first Primary Curriculum for Character Education. He says:

'At Kehelland School our Primary Character Curriculum aims to develop a range of virtues in children which we believe are vital to human flourishing. We expect children to learn mathematical concepts and the associated vocabulary to help them develop academically and I believe it is also essential that we teach the virtues and virtuous vocabulary to help them develop and strengthen their characters.'

The children at Kehelland School say:

'Virtues are the good parts of our characters!'
'Virtues help us to respect others.'

'The Virtues Project helps me to be the best that I can be.'

'Virtues make the school a happier place!'

'Virtues help you to learn and have a happier life!'

There are numerous organisations that support character education and these are two of note. Character.org is a US-based nonprofit, nonpartisan, nonsectarian coalition of organisations and individuals committed to fostering effective character education. Its mission is 'Providing leadership and advocacy for character worldwide'. Its vision is that, 'young people everywhere be educated, inspired and empowered to be ethical and compassionate citizens'. (https://character.org).

Kindness.org is a nonprofit digital platform dedicated to promoting kindness around the world. At kindness.org they 'believe that kindness transcends difference' and that:

Kindness is. . .

All around us

Impactful and measurable

Infinite with imagination

Serious, and seriously fun

Sometimes surprising

A choice for everyone (https://kindness.org)

Kindness has become a central value in many schools and kindness.org offers resources and strategies to embed kindness in school life, and in our personal and work lives. Research has shown that when we demonstrate kindness to others there are elevated levels of dopamine in the brain and we actually feel better as a result; being kind boosts our happiness. Research into the effects of kindness is continuing and kindness.org has partnered with Oxford University to study, investigate and explore kindness all over the globe.

We see an increasing development of service learning and social action projects for children in our schools, and increasing numbers of organisations online that build character, and encourage children to join their efforts to make a positive difference.

PAUSE FOR REFLECTION

What benefits does integrating character education bring to your class and school?

What service learning and social action projects are your students already involved in?

How do service learning and social action projects enhance your students' character, knowledge and understanding?

We recognise our differences and we also share common human values

While different cultures promote different values there are also shared values that are widely recognised as important for our common humanity. The United Nations Declaration of Human Rights (UNDHR) and the United Nations Convention on the Rights of the Child (UNCRC) underscore the value of all cultures, languages and religions, and the rights of all people, including children, to enjoy and practise them freely.

In 2003 Kofi Annan, then Secretary-General of the United Nations, delivered a speech at Tübingen University in Germany. He asserted his belief that, yes, there are universal values:

'The values of peace, freedom, social progress, equal rights and human dignity enshrined in the Charter of the United Nations and in the Universal Declaration of Human Rights, are no less valid today than when, over half a century ago, those documents were drafted by many different nations and cultures.'

He stated that, 'they were more acutely needed, in this age of globalisation, than ever before'. This continues to be true today.

At the Global Futures Initiative in 2015 Professor John M Kline, responding to the Georgetown Faculty on the Greatest Development Challenge of the Next Decade, identified the task ahead as shared human values. He stated that:

the greatest development challenge of the next decade is the identification and promotion of shared human values essential to build a true global society. Sustainable and equitable global development will not spring spontaneously from macro forces of political and economic competition. Neither will it arise from piecemeal responses to discrete problems or threats. Global development requires a normative commitment to shared values that recognize and enhance the international community's common welfare.

(Global Futures Initiative, 2015)

Our shared human values can also be seen in the Golden Rule, 'Do unto others as you would have them do unto you'. It exists in some form in major religions and belief systems throughout the world, and is the foundation upon which many of our laws are based. It states that we should treat others as we wish to be treated and is essentially about love and kindness.

The love and kindness of children was beautifully expressed following the earthquake in L'Aquila, Italy, in 2009. As Junior School Principal at the International School of Florence I worked with the Student Council to support the children's initiatives. We met shortly after the tragedy and the students immediately began talking about the ways they wanted to help the children of L'Aquila. We talked about what they might need and the children suggested toys, books, food, clothing, glasses and medicine. After a few minutes one young boy added something else. He said they needed love. We all thought it was a beautiful idea and that it was true. We talked about how we could do that; send our love to the children of L'Aquila. The children thought that each class could send cards and messages of hope. They planned and organised the project, visiting each classroom to explain it to the students and their teachers. In the end we amassed a touching collection of cards and watercolour paintings, tied with coloured ribbon. The images showed children holding hands, holding hearts, sunshine, flowers and rainbows, and some of the messages read: 'You are not alone. / *Non siete soli.*', 'We are with you. / *Noi siamo con voi.*', 'Don't give up hope! / *Non perdere la speranza.*' and 'We are sending you love from Florence. / *Con amore da Firenze.*'

One of our colleagues had a relative who worked for *la Croce Rossa* (the Red Cross) and I hand delivered this package of love to its office on the River Arno. It was to be taken to L'Aquila with the next truckload of supplies. We never knew if our messages were received, and hoped they were and brought comfort to others. It was a powerful learning experience about kindness and empathy, and doing a good turn because it was a kind thing to do, and not for recognition. The children also worked with their teachers to organise a collection of supplies for the Red Cross, calling their project *Dai Bambini Per I Bambini*, 'From the Children to the Children'.

We know that cultures are complex and diverse. It is important to be aware that while there may be shared values, there may also be culturally different ways of expressing them. For example, respect may be a shared value, however in some cultures respect may mean telling the truth while in others, avoiding the truth so that someone can save face may be seen as respectful. As with all cultural learning and interaction we cannot assume that others think and behave in the same way we do. However, it is important to recognise our shared values that unite our common humanity in essential ways.

Beliefs, values and attitudes to develop for intercultural understanding

Drawing on the work of UNESCO, Oxfam and others, as is reflected in my *Framework for Developing Intercultural Understanding* (Rader, 2016), I put forward the following beliefs, values and attitudes for intercultural understanding that I believe are critical to live and work effectively and harmoniously with all others.

Compassion and empathy

Compassion is understanding and caring when someone is in need. We can help children see how developing compassion for oneself and others contributes to a kinder world. Empathy is the ability to understand another person's feelings, situation or perspective. Compassion and empathy are human responses to the needs and suffering of others. When we understand another person's situation we are usually moved to experience empathy. Empathy often leads to action and inclusion yet this is not a given and needs to be encouraged. This attitude extends to how we interact with and care for living things and the environment.

Caring and kindness

Caring is helping others and treating them with kindness and respect. Caring includes caring for oneself, others, our community and our world. Kindness reflects a generosity of spirit and is the action we take to make people's lives and our world better. Kindness reflects the power of human beings to be the best they can be and see the best in each other. When we model and intentionally nurture kindness in our schools, children can learn the powerful effect it has on ourselves and others.

Open-mindedness

Open-mindedness is an acceptance of different perspectives, ideas, ways of doing things and ways of being. The wording in the IB mission statement says, 'These programmes encourage students across the world to become active, compassionate and lifelong learners who understand that *other people, with their differences, can also be right*'. (IB website, italics added). Through presenting and inviting different perspectives children can learn that there is no one right way, and to honour their own thoughts and ideas, and those of others.

Curiosity and interest in others

Curiosity is wondering and wanting to find out. It is what moves us to ask questions and find answers. Children are naturally curious and we can build on their curiosity to develop an interest in learning about other cultures, languages and people. Children can learn to approach difference with curiosity and interest instead of with fear and uncertainty. In this way difference becomes normalised and something positive.

Appreciation and respect for diversity

We recognise that diversity enriches our lives and we value the diversity other cultures, languages and ways of being in the world bring. While the primary focus in this book is on cultural

PAUSE FOR REFLECTION

Consider the ways you model our shared beliefs, values and attitudes for your students.

How are they embedded in the life of your classroom and school?

How could you do so more intentionally?

Concepts featured in the learning engagements

Our beliefs, values and attitudes directly influence our behaviour and actions

Our beliefs, values and attitudes not only affect the way we interact with others but also the choices we make and the way we live our lives. We can help children reflect on the beliefs, values and attitudes they hold and see how they guide their choices, interests, actions and behaviours.

Our shared values unite us in our common humanity

Through the UNDHR and the UNCRC we can identify values that are shared by peoples around the world that honour and respect our common humanity. It is essential for children to begin to understand that regardless of our differences there are values that we all share. As educators we need to provide continuous opportunities to discuss and reinforce this understanding. It is through understanding that, regardless of our differences, we are all human beings with similar hopes and dreams who desire the same things; a peaceful world, love and safety for our families. That is what can move us to have compassion and empathy, and to look after each other.

A belief in the positive difference we each can make and an attitude of optimism are essential for creating a hopeful future

Each one of us has gifts to bring into the world, whoever we are and wherever we are. As children learn this and we as educators provide opportunities for them to experience the positive effects of their efforts, they are empowered to help make a positive difference in the world. With our support children can learn that they can show leadership in many different ways, and help create a better future.

We aim to actively find ways to live our beliefs, values and attitudes throughout our lives

Our beliefs, values and attitudes guide us throughout our lives and influence the ways we respond to an ever-changing world. As we develop intercultural understanding our positive beliefs, values and attitudes are increasingly reflected in the way we live our lives, take positive action and engage with others. We can encourage children to see the importance of living aligned with our values.

Our beliefs, values and attitudes may change and/or stay the same

There are core beliefs, values and attitudes that we learn as children. As we live our lives, and grow and develop greater knowledge, understanding and awareness of the world we develop beliefs, values and attitudes that contribute to a peaceful, just and sustainable world. Due to teachings and circumstances negative beliefs, values and attitudes can also be developed. It is essential that we teach children beliefs, values and attitudes that enhance our humanity and to resist those than are born of fear and ignorance, and harm others.

Learning outcomes

Learners will:

- Develop greater appreciation and respect for diversity.
- Develop greater compassion and empathy.
- Cultivate caring and kindness.
- Develop open-mindedness.
- Develop genuine curiosity about and interest in other people, their cultures and lives.
- Develop tolerance and respect for others and their differences.
- Cultivate a belief in human dignity and human rights for all people.
- Begin to stand up for social justice and equity for oneself and others.
- Begin to assume responsibility for making a positive difference in our world.
- Begin to demonstrate confidence and courage when presented with new experiences.
- Develop an enjoyment and appreciation of different cultural experiences, and begin to seek them out.

References

Annan, K (2003) Speech, Tübingen University: www.un.org/press/en/2003/sgsm9076.doc.htm

Brooks, D (2015) *The Road to Character*. New York, NY: Random House.

character.org: http://character.org

IBO: www.ibo.org/about-the-ib/mission (accessed May 2017).

Kehelland Village School, cited in *The Guardian* (2013): www.theguardian.com/teacher-network/teacher-blog/2013/mar/28/character-education-teaching-values

kindness.org: www.kindness.org (accessed April 2017).

Kline, J (2015) Global Futures Initiative Speech: http://globalfutures.georgetown.edu/responses/the-task-ahead-shared-human-values (accessed January 2018).

Oxfam GB (2015) *Education for Global Citizenship: A Guide for Schools*. www.oxfam.org.uk/education/global-citizenship/global-citizenship-guides (accessed January 2016).

Tough, P (2012) *How Children Succeed: Grit, Curiosity and the Hidden Power of Character*. New York, NY: Houghton Mifflin Harcourt.

UNESCO (2015) *Education 2030: Incheon Declaration and Framework for Action Towards Inclusive and Equitable Quality Education and Lifelong Learning for All*. Paris, France.

University of Birmingham Jubilee Centre: www.jubileecentre.ac.uk (accessed May 2017).

Values-based Education: www.valuesbasededucation.com (accessed April 2017).

Virtues Project: www.virtuesproject.com/homepage.html (accessed May 2017).

The Golden Rule

by Ilene Cooper
Illustrated by Gabi Swiatkowska

Synopsis

The Golden Rule can be found in almost every religion and culture in the world. In this beautifully written and illustrated picture book a grandfather teaches his grandson about the Golden Rule and together they discuss its meaning. He explains that the Golden Rule, 'Do unto others as you would have them do unto you', means to treat people the way you would like to be treated. He shares versions of the Golden Rule that are found in Christianity, Judaism, Islam, Hinduism, Buddhism and the Shawnee Tribe Tradition. They talk about ways the boy would like to be treated and how he would not want to be treated, and they discuss how he can practise the Golden Rule. I love the grandfather's explanation that, 'it's golden because it's so valuable, and a way of living your life that's so simple, it shines'.

This book could be used at the beginning of the school year when you and your students are creating your Essential Agreements for how you will learn, work and play together throughout the year.

Learning outcomes

Learners will:

- Develop greater appreciation and respect for diversity.
- Develop greater compassion and empathy.
- Cultivate caring and kindness.
- Develop open-mindedness.
- Develop genuine curiosity about and interest in other people, their cultures and lives.
- Begin to stand up to injustice, and speak out and take action.
- Begin to assume responsibility for making a positive difference in our world.

Pre-reading activities

- Introduce the book and ask your students if they have ever heard of the Golden Rule. Invite them to share what they know about it. Together establish that it means to treat people the way you would like to be treated.

Post-reading activities

- Invite any questions or comments the children have about the conversation the boy has with his grandfather. Is there anything new they learned about the Golden Rule? Are there any connections they made?

- The grandfather says that the Golden Rule is simple but may not always be easy. Explain that the Golden Rule requires practice and takes time to become part of how we live our lives.

  Discuss how we practise the Golden Rule here in our classroom. Chart the children's responses by creating a double-sided list of the ways the children *do* practise the Golden Rule on one side, and other ways they *could* practise the Golden Rule in your classroom on the other. Young children may give examples such as take turns, share toys, line up without pushing or play nicely. Older children might suggest including everyone, respecting others or standing up for others if they are teased or bullied. Add similar practices for outside the classroom such as during lunch, playtime or on the bus.

- The boy asks his grandfather how he can start to practise the Golden Rule and he tells him to begin by using his imagination, to imagine how someone else feels. Explain to your students that this is the way we begin to develop empathy, when we can imagine what a situation is like from another person's point of view. Empathy can move us to help someone who feels sad or is in need.

  They talk about how someone feels when he or she is new, and how the boy would feel and what would make him feel better. Discuss how children can show empathy for someone who is new and doesn't speak the same language. Suggestions might include smile at the new child, ask him or her to play, read a book together, look at a book in his or her language and ask him or her to sit with you at lunch. Include their suggestions in a plan for welcoming new students to your class.

  Invite the children to share examples of when someone has shown empathy towards them. Examples might include a time they fell in the playground, someone was teasing them and others stood up for them, or someone comforted them when they were sad. Continue sharing examples of when they have shown empathy towards someone else.

- Discuss: How would you describe the boy and why? (curious, caring, a thinker, reflective, and had empathy). Have the children recall evidence from the text to support their thinking. In what ways are you like the boy? What qualities do you think you need to practise the Golden Rule? (kind, caring, observant, thoughtful).

- Create a class book where each child draws and writes about how they practise the Golden Rule at home, in your class, in your school and in the community.

- Practise the Golden Rule through acting out scenarios. Generate a list of scenarios with the students where they could practise the Golden Rule. Here are some ideas:

  A child is new to the class

  A child is teased

  A child loses a special toy

  A child falls down in the playground

Suggested follow-up activities

- The grandfather poses two big and important questions to think about. He wonders how things would change if everyone lived by the Golden Rule. He also asks, 'What if countries lived by the Golden Rule?' Discuss the first question as a class or in small groups.

- Have the children write *If. . .Then* poems following the pattern below.

  If everyone in our class and school lived by the Golden Rule. . .

  Then our school would be a kinder place

  Then people would listen to each other

Then. . .

Then. . .

Then. . .

- Living our lives according to the Golden Rule takes practice and can be reinforced by teaching it to others. Have your students explain the Golden Rule to the children in other classes and interview them about how they practise the Golden Rule. Their findings could be displayed for the school community on notice boards or large TV screens.

- The boy and his grandfather also talk about how the boy would not want to be treated and how he feels when he is teased or bullied. Have your students create an anti-bullying video, guidebook or website for other children including ways to speak out and take action if they or others are bullied.

- On the last page of the book the grandfather tells his grandson that practising the Golden Rule begins with you. Discuss the idea of the personal responsibility we all have for making a positive difference in our world. Have your students write or draw about a time when they took responsibility to make a positive difference at home, in your class, in your school and/ or in the community.

  Discuss the responsibility we all have for ourselves and each other, and how responsibility leads to social action. Have your students think of initiatives they might undertake to improve your school. Alternatively have your students research projects they would like to support locally and/or globally.

  Have your students write a personal pledge listing the ways they will practise the Golden Rule. It is helpful to use the format:

  I would like. . .   So I will. . .

  For example:

  I would like to be included in games at playtime. . . So I will ask others to play. . .

  Have them share their list with a partner and display the pledges in your classroom.

Links with learning outcomes in other chapters

This book links with learning outcomes in the following chapter:

Chapter 4: 'Exploring culture and language'

Learners will:
Gain knowledge of different cultural beliefs including secular and faith-based practices.
Develop greater appreciation and respect for cultural and linguistic diversity.

- The author's endnotes provide background information about the Golden Rule in the major religions mentioned in the text. Have your students research the Golden Rule in their religions or belief systems. Invite parents or caregivers in to school to talk about how they practise the Golden Rule.

- The artwork on each page is inspired by the original art the artist associates with each faith. Invite parents, caregivers and colleagues to share examples of artwork or images they may have from their faith traditions or that they have collected on their travels. Collaborate with your art teacher and have your students create an art book with samples of artwork from different cultures represented in the book.

Notes

Author and parent Dana Williams says teaching tolerance to children must begin with the Golden Rule but go beyond it. She suggests parents be honest, lead by example and speak out. I believe these suggestions are equally important for teachers, too. You can read her article *Beyond the Golden Rule* at www.tolerance.org/magazine/fall-2005/beyond-the-golden-rule and download her publication *Beyond the Golden Rule: A Parent's Guide to Preventing and Responding to Prejudice* on the teaching tolerance website, www.tolerance.org/sites/default/files/general/beyond_golden_rule.pdf.

Introduction

I have long been a fan of Little Pickle Press (now March4th Inc.) and I applaud their founding mission and practice. 'Little Pickle Press is dedicated to helping parents and educators cultivate conscious, responsible, little people by stimulating explorations of the meaningful topics of their generation through a variety of media, technologies and techniques.' Their books are published and distributed in an environmentally-friendly manner, and through their collaborative partnerships and outreach programmes, they actively enrich the lives of children and provide books for children in need.

I particularly admire the *What Does It Mean to Be. . .?*® series written by Rana DiOrio, the founder of Little Pickle Press and now CEO and Chairman of March 4th Inc., and I have included many of the titles published in this book. While I have placed *What Does It Mean to Be Global?* in Chapter 6, it addresses all of the components of the *Framework for Developing Intercultural Understanding* (Rader, 2016).

You will find two lesson plans for this book: Reception–Year 2 followed by Year 3–Year 6.

Lesson plan: Reception–Year 2

What Does It Mean to Be Global?
by Rana DiOrio

Synopsis

In this book the author illustrates what it means to be a global citizen. It is simply written, yet contains powerful ideas to explore further and think more deeply about with children. It provides an excellent springboard to begin to develop both the disposition and competence of intercultural understanding in the young children we teach, which is at the heart of global citizenship.

This lesson plan is written for children, aged four to six years-old. At this age we are affirming the rich diversity they bring to the classroom, building on the children's life experiences both in and out of school, and creating new multicultural and multilingual experiences in the context of the classroom and school life. This book is best used once you have a range of shared multicultural experiences you can draw from. You may have recorded these learning engagements through photographs, and video and/or audio clips, which can be used as concrete examples of ways you value the diversity the children and their families bring. You will likely refer back to them often throughout the school year.

This lesson plan can be adapted for the class and age you teach. This book can also be used beautifully as the basis for a year-long enquiry into developing global-mindedness, or over weeks or months as part of a unit. The ideas and images on each page invite discussion, and you can follow the children's observations and wonderings, and support their curiosity to see what further learning engagements emerge.

Learning outcomes

Young learners will:

- Discuss some of the beliefs, values, attitudes, and behaviours of globally-minded people
- Identify ways they are globally-minded and choose new ones to try

- Develop greater appreciation and respect for different cultures, languages, and diversity

- Develop an attitude of open-mindedness to the values and traditions of others

- Develop genuine curiosity and interest in learning about other people, their cultures and lives

- Develop an enjoyment and appreciation of different cultural experiences, and begin to seek them out.

Pre-reading activities

- Begin by affirming that our world, our countries, our communities and our families are multicultural and multilingual. Acknowledge that the children and adults in your class, school and community come from different countries and cultural backgrounds, and speak different languages. Affirm the unique backgrounds and diversity of you and your students, explaining that we each have cultural influences in our lives from our families and cultural heritage, and our life experiences.

  Share photographs, and play video and/or audio clips you have of your class and the classroom that reflect the children's families, the different cultures and languages that are valued and celebrated, and the ways you honour diversity and inclusion. These examples might include children sharing books in different languages, playing and listening to music or singing songs from different cultures and in different languages, trying foods from different cultures, playing games or playing with toys from different cultures, learning about and celebrating different festivals and traditions, multilingual signage and your multilingual library. The children will enjoy recounting these experiences with you and this provides a concrete, personal and multisensory way to do so. Alternatively, you could use images from books and other sources to notice the ways children and adults celebrate and appreciate languages and cultures, and all forms of diversity.

- Lead a discussion about how we are all part of our community here in our classroom and at our school, in our town or city, and in our wider world or global community, where people from different cultures and who speak different languages learn and work together. Discuss some of the ways we interact with people from different cultures in our lives. These might include the classmates we learn and play with, our teachers in the school, our neighbours, local shopkeepers, people we meet when we travel, family and friends we communicate with around the world through technology, etc.

- Have your students think about what it means to be global; to think and to live our lives in a global way; one that is curious and appreciates the differences there are in our world. Talk about how we are all learning to be more global. What do you think it looks like when people are global? What might we see them doing? What do you think it sounds like when people are global? What might we hear them saying?

Introduce the book, *What Does It Mean to Be Global?* by Rana DiOrio, where the author shares her ideas about what it means to be global. Invite the children's ideas and discuss the question, What do *you* think it means to be global?

Begin a simple chart on *Being Global* and list the ways you and your students are global; are curious and appreciate diversity and differences. Include examples from your photographs, video and audio, the children's lives and any other ideas the children may have. Post the photographs alongside the words where possible, to support them with a visual image.

I suggest you first read the book through once without much oral discussion, responding to what the children notice, so the children can inwardly reflect on the ideas presented. Let the children know that as you read they may see some of the things you talked about, and things they do at home or outside of school, or that you do at school.

Choose a few pages to re-read, starting with being curious. Discuss the ideas and illustrations, which are thoughtfully detailed, and respond to your students' observations, connections, questions and wonderings, identifying and affirming the ways they are global and the advantages of this disposition. You can continue reading and discussing this book over time as best meets the needs of your class.

Post-reading activities

- Have the children recount some of the ways the children in the book are global. Add any new ideas they have about ways to be global to the initial chart.

- Have your students create a *Global Me!* map where the children draw and write to illustrate the ways they are global. You can draw on the class photographs you have displayed, your classroom routines and experiences such as when you listen to music from different countries, celebrate the children's festivals and greet each other in the languages of the class at Morning Circle Time. The children can refer back to the chart you started and include other ideas they have. Plan time for them to share their maps with their classmates and display them for others to enjoy. You may wish to leave them up so the children can add to their maps over time. Young children could possibly work on their maps with their family at home.

Alternatively, you could create a notice board called *We're Growing Global* and add to it throughout the year, including the children's drawings and posting relevant photographs.

Suggested follow-up activities

- Students can share what they have learned about different cultures and languages, and about being global with their buddies and/or other classes and years within the school.

- Invite the children and their parents to teach the class about a cultural practice or tradition in their families. It could involve experiencing a special meal, the ways birthdays are celebrated or learning a song or dance from their culture. Have the families also talk about the history and beliefs behind the practice, the meaning it holds for them, and how it makes them feel. This underscores the heart connection our cultural practices hold so we can understand their importance.

- You may choose to write a class poem on the ways you as a class, are becoming more global.

    Example: *We used to. . . But now. . .*

    We used to only greet each other in English. . . But now we greet each other in Hindi, Arabic, and ____ too.

    We used to listen to Western music in the morning. . . But now we listen to Persian and ____ music, too.

    We used to only sing in English. . . But now we sing in Chinese, German and____ too.

    We used to eat the foods we know. . . But now we try foods from different places.

    We used to. . . But now. . .

These ideas could be shared with the school community through a student-created and student-led assembly, where the children also share poems and songs in different languages, and/or music, art projects, dances etc. from different cultures.

What Does It Mean to Be Global?
by Rana DiOrio

Synopsis

In this book the author illustrates what it means to be a global citizen. It is simply written, yet contains powerful ideas to explore further and think more deeply about with children. It provides an excellent springboard to develop both the disposition and competence of intercultural understanding in the children we teach, which is at the heart of global citizenship.

This lesson plan can be used on its own and adapted for your particular class. This book can also be used beautifully as the basis for a year-long enquiry into developing global-mindedness, or over weeks or months as part of a unit. Following the main lesson plan I have included suggestions based on each page of the book that delve more deeply into each of the ideas presented, and invite student-led learning. Please read the Introduction at the beginning of the What Does It Mean to Be Global? lesson plan for Reception–Year 2.

Learning outcomes

Learners will:

- Reflect on what it means to be global, and identify some of the beliefs, values, attitudes, and behaviours globally-minded people.
- Identify ways they are globally-minded and choose new ones to try.
- Develop greater appreciation and respect for different cultures, languages and diversity.
- Develop an attitude of open-mindedness to the values and traditions of others.
- Develop genuine curiosity and interest in learning about other people, their cultures and lives.
- Develop an enjoyment and appreciation of different cultural experiences, and begin to seek them out.

Pre-reading activities

- Begin by affirming that our world, our countries, our communities and our families are multicultural and multilingual. Acknowledge that the children and adults in your class, school and community come from different countries and cultural backgrounds, and speak different languages. Affirm the unique backgrounds and diversity of you and your students, explaining that we each have cultural influences in our lives from our families, our cultural heritage and our life experiences. As described in the lesson plan for Reception–Year 2 you could begin with sharing class photographs, and video and audio clips to elicit from the children the ways your class is global. Alternatively, you could use images from books and other sources to notice the ways children and adults are global.
- Explain that we are part of our local community and we are also part of our wider world or global community, wherever we may live. Discuss some of the ways we interact with people

Lesson plan: Reception–Year 6

Each Kindness

by Jacqueline Woodson
Illustrations by E B Lewis

Synopsis

This is a powerful story about a girl called Chloe who is unkind to Maya, a new girl in her class. When Maya arrives at school she looks different from the other children, as her clothes are old and ragged, and inappropriate for winter. Maya tries to befriend Chloe but Chloe turns away and ignores her. Maya continues to reach out to Chloe and her friends but they exclude her, and make fun of her clothes, her shoes and the strange food she brings for lunch. One day Maya does not return to school. The class teacher, Ms Albert, brings a bowl of water and a stone to class and talks with the children about kindness. She demonstrates how each act of kindness, no matter how small, ripples out into the world. Chloe realises that the way she treated Maya was unkind and a lost opportunity to show kindness, and waits for her to return. One day Ms Albert tells the class that Maya will not be coming back and Chloe is filled with regret about the kindness she had never shown.

This story provides an excellent opportunity to help your students develop empathy and kindness, understand difference and explore their feelings when they encounter difference. Chloe and her friends continually laughed at Maya, made fun of her and excluded her, which is a form of bullying and is vital to address.

Learning outcomes

Learners will:

- Develop greater appreciation and respect for diversity.
- Develop greater compassion and empathy for others who are different.
- Cultivate caring and kindness.
- Develop open-mindedness towards others who are different from us.
- Develop genuine curiosity about and interest in other people, their cultures and lives.
- Develop tolerance and respect for others and their differences.
- Cultivate a belief in human dignity and human rights for all people.
- Begin to stand up to injustice, and speak out and take action (see Chapter 7 activity).
- Begin to assume responsibility for making a positive difference in our world.
- Begin to demonstrate confidence and courage when presented with new experiences.

Pre-reading activities

- Initiate a discussion about kindness; what it means to be kind, what it looks like when we are kind, and how it feels when we are kind and when someone is kind to us. Draw on examples from the kindness you and your students observe in your class, school, homes and community. Continue the discussion to address being unkind.

Explain that this story helps us understand the impact of kindness on others and ourselves, and the effect it has when we are unkind.

Post-reading activities

- This story has a painful ending as the problem is left unresolved and some children may have strong feelings. They may have experienced or witnessed a similar situation. Invite the children's questions and comments, and be prepared to discuss painful experiences and sadness. Discuss the author's purpose and messages. What did you learn about kindness? What did you learn about withholding it?

- Why do you think Chloe did not respond to Maya? Possible answers might be because she was different and Chloe felt uncomfortable or maybe afraid, she had prejudice about people who are poor and she thought the other kids would laugh at her.

- Ask the children to put themselves in Maya's shoes, and discuss how she might feel. Explain that this is empathy, which helps us to be kind and caring, and reach out to and respond to others. Through a guided conversation explore the prejudice that some people have about people who are poor. What are some of their mistaken assumptions? Do you think the children would have responded differently if Maya dressed differently and her family had more money? Establish that some children and their families may not have much money or the same things other people have, but they are children like you, with feelings like you, and they want to be treated with kindness just like you do. They want to make and have friends, too. Why do you think people judge others who are different than they are?

  How can we challenge and resist prejudice we may have? This is a good opportunity to talk about having confidence and courage to learn about people and places without judgement when we are faced with a new situation.

- With older children you might also discuss the possible reasons Maya's family left so quickly and after such a short time. This could lead to recognising the challenges and developing empathy for migrant workers and/or families who cannot find permanent work.

- Discuss the ripple effect of kindness the children learned about from Ms Albert. Together create a list of ways you and your students will show kindness to each other, and let it ripple through your class and school. These could be made into a banner for your classroom or included in your Essential Agreements.

  Based on the book, *Kids' Random Acts of Kindness,* edited by Roslyn Carter, have your students create a similar class book. Have the children write about and illustrate an act of kindness they showed another person or saw done by someone else. Consider ways these pages could be shared with the whole school; perhaps displayed on TV screens to inspire acts of kindness throughout the school community. Consider sharing random acts of kindness you have done and seen as well. You may wish to also read and discuss *What Does It Mean to Be Kind?* by Rana DiOrio.

- Discuss kind and respectful ways to welcome someone who is new. The children stared at Maya and most were silent when Ms Albert asked them to say hello. How could the children and their teacher have treated Maya with dignity and respect, and been more welcoming? Together create a plan for how your class can welcome new students to your class and school.

Continue the discussion and discuss the role of the teacher. Why did she wait so long to talk to the class about kindness? Why didn't she act if she saw that Maya was excluded or being bullied? Explain that sometimes adults are unaware of bullying or other problems, and children can have an important role in raising concerns and making a positive difference.

Suggested follow-up activities

- You may wish to introduce the idea of creating a class Awareness Log (discussed in Chapter 10) where children record and share acts of kindness they observe among their classmates.

- When we are unkind it is important to make things right with the other person. Chloe did not have the chance to do that and her throat was filled with all the things she wished she would have said to Maya. Have the children write a letter to Maya from Chloe even though she could not send it. What would she say to her? This can be done as a whole-class shared writing activity with younger children. The children can role-play in pairs each playing the role of Chloe reading her letter and Maya responding.

- How could Chloe move past her regret? She could have compassion for herself, accept that she made a mistake and choose to show kindness in the future. Have you ever been unkind and how did you make things right? Discuss ways we can move past our mistakes and learn from them for the future.

- Discuss exclusion and inclusion, and what both look and feel like. Have the children write double-sided poems, one about exclusion and one about inclusion.

- With older students you might view the video *We Dine Together* (see Appendix B), a news story about students at a Boca Raton High School in Florida who started a programme where no student eats lunch alone. Support your students' ideas on ways to create an inclusive community in your class and school.

- Consider ways to cultivate gratitude in your class. You could designate a notice board where children post pictures or messages of their gratitude, which reflect acts of kindness they and others have shown. Some teachers have their students keep a gratitude journal to write about the things they are grateful for on a daily or weekly basis.

Links with learning outcomes in other chapters

This book links with learning outcomes in the following chapters:

Chapter 7: 'Engaging with difference'

Learners will:
Begin to learn about stereotypes, prejudice, discrimination and their impact.
Develop the ability to recognise, challenge and resist stereotypes, prejudice and discrimination.
Begin to understand bullying and its effect on others.
Begin to stand up to injustice, and speak out and take action.
Seek commonalities, and learn about 'reaching in' and 'reaching out'.
Explore the emotions associated with discomfort, and healthy ways to address them.
Begin to develop self-monitoring and self-management skills.
Consider ways to engage with others who are different from themselves.

- Chloe and the other children judged Maya based on the second-hand clothes she wore. Initiate a conversation about stereotypes, prejudice and discrimination, and why they are wrong (see the *Amazing Grace* lesson plan in Chapter 7).

- Initiate a discussion about feeling discomfort, particularly when we are faced with a new and different situation. How do some people respond to the discomfort they experience with difference? Chloe responded by avoiding, ignoring and excluding Maya. What could she have done instead? What would you have done if you were Chloe?

- Initiate a discussion about bullying and what it is and its effects on the victim and bully. Have your students identify the ways Chloe, Kendra and Sophie bullied Maya. Every day they whispered about her, laughed at her clothes, her shoes, the strange food she brought for lunch and they intentionally excluded and ignored her. How could the other children in the class have stood up for Maya? How could Maya have found her voice and spoken out, too? Have your students act out one of the scenes in the book where Maya is laughed at or excluded, giving everyone including Maya a chance to speak out and stand up to the kids who are being unkind. Stress the importance of responding in a way that is strong, confident and respectful. Excellent resources can be found on www.welcomingschools.org and www.tolerance.org.

- Maya 'reached in' to her new class when she brought her jacks, cards and doll to share with the other children. How could the other children have looked for things they had in common and 'reached out' to her? They might have played card games and tricks, brought their games to play with her and included her at lunch and playtime.

Chapter 8: 'Developing essential intercultural, interpersonal and life skills'

Learners will:
Become more observant and reflect on what they notice.

- Chloe and the other children didn't see Maya as being more than poor, and try to get to know her. What can you observe about what Maya is like from the story? She is brave, confident, kind, friendly, likes to play, and shares her toys and games. When we take time to observe other people and situations we can learn more about them rather than judging them and making assumptions. Have your students tell about a time they were observant and did not make assumptions about another person.

Notes

It is important to listen to children and honour their thinking, concerns and worries in a non-evaluative way. When children ask questions or make comments about differences they observe it may feel awkward or embarrassing. However, we need to respond with accurate information that affirms the dignity and value of others. We need to take their feelings seriously and talk through their fear or discomfort. This is essential if we are to help children see past differences and engage with others who may be different than they are. It is important to ask students not to use people's names or identify anyone when sharing.

Two areas of particular concern

Bullying continues to be a problem in schools and communities, and online through social media. Many schools have adopted anti-bullying programmes and actively teach children about being a bystander, upstander or changemaker. No Bully offers valuable resources to educators who wish to counter bullying in their schools and suggests activities such as *Just Like Me* to build compassion, and how to hold a peace summit at your school. You can visit its website at www.nobully.org.

We have seen an increase in inflammatory speech in communities around the world. We can help teach children the value of freedom of speech and the responsibility that comes along with exercising this right. Our words are powerful and can have a positive or negative impact on others. Help your students recognise and understand how their words can help or hurt others. It is also important to help children to understand that the right to freedom of speech does not give anyone the right to humiliate, defame and degrade others. We can help guide children to live their lives with integrity, and aim to resolve conflicts in moral and ethical ways that respect others.

With mutual respect, and a commitment to effective communication and conflict resolution we can all learn to defuse conflicts and find viable solutions when conflicts arise. When we defuse conflicts we can focus on our commonalities and interact with others who are different from us.

Addressing stereotypes, prejudice, discrimination and racism

We first need to acknowledge that stereotypes, prejudice, discrimination and racism exist in order to prevent and reduce them. We all hold stereotypes and prejudice to some degree and it is with self-awareness and self-knowledge that we can learn about their impact on ourselves and others, and begin to recognise, challenge, resist, and speak out and take action against them. We must first learn to do this ourselves so we can then teach children to do the same.

The following definitions provide a shared understanding of the terms *stereotype, prejudice, discrimination* and *racism* as we consider how to address them together.

A *stereotype* is a widely held and oversimplified image or idea of a particular group of people. Stereotypes are the basis of prejudice and discrimination.

Prejudice is a preconceived opinion that is not based on reason or actual experience. Prejudice is based on stereotypes and is usually associated with negative emotions.

Discrimination is the unjust or prejudicial treatment of different categories of people, such as on the grounds of race, ethnicity, age, gender, religion or socioeconomic status.

Racism is prejudice, discrimination, and/or antagonism directed against someone of a different race based on the belief that one's own race is superior. In her anti-bias work Stacey York (2016) defines racism simply as 'prejudice plus power'. Racism is both individual and institutional. It is reflected in the way we interact with others, and in the policies, procedures and practices of an organisation.

The concept of *white privilege* is part of the discourse on race and racism and I believe it is important to understand its role in how we think about race. 'White privilege exists when white people, who may have been taught that racism is something that puts some people at a disadvantage, are not taught to see the corresponding advantage that their own colour brings them' (Cushner et al., 2015). White privilege is largely unconscious and most white people do not understand its impact. However, it is critical that we as educators understand the impact of white privilege if we are to fully understand racism and help counter it. An excellent overview of white privilege can be found on www.tolerance.org excerpted from *White Anti-Racist Activism: A Personal Roadmap* by Jennifer R. Holladay, M. S.

There is no biological basis for prejudice or racism. It is considered a social construct that is learned beginning when children are young. Children begin to recognise differences as infants and form attitudes about those differences as they grow and develop. Children learn stereotypes and prejudice through what they see and hear from other children and adults, from the media and from their social groups.

Advances in neuroscience have enabled us to learn more about how the human brain functions and research in the field of social psychology continues to be conducted to help us better understand prejudice. Studies suggest that prejudice is an emotional response rather than a cognitive response. We make unconscious judgements about others quickly, based on the attitudes we hold about difference. Researchers have found evidence that there is activity in the amygdala, the emotional centre of our brain that registers a fear response when individuals are presented with images of those who are from different races. (Lieff, 2014). However, prejudice can be prevented, recognised, challenged and resisted.

PAUSE FOR REFLECTION

Can you think of times when you have observed stereotypes, prejudice, discrimination or racism among the children you teach?

You may have felt uncomfortable and unsure of how to respond.

What was your response? What kind of support would you like to address these areas with confidence?

These are challenging topics for all of us. These may also be uncomfortable topics for us to address with children, parents and colleagues; however, we need to address them intentionally if we are to prevent and reduce prejudice and racism in our schools, communities and world. We can support each other in being bold and deliberate, and taking the necessary steps to address them. It is helpful to be informed about relevant historical, social, political and educational issues, and keep current with local and world affairs. Most importantly we need to have confidence and courage to enter into constructive dialogue about them.

We cannot ignore disturbing comments that children may make such as those that appear racist, anti-Semitic or Islamist, sexist or homophobic. We can help and encourage children to examine the assumptions behind their comments and correct any misconceptions. As educators we must talk with children about differences and clarify misinformation. We must also help children think critically and learn to evaluate the images and information they see and hear in the media, and on social media, that may spread misinformation and create stereotypes.

We need to talk with children about what exclusion looks like and how it feels. And it is equally important to talk with children about what inclusion looks like, how it feels, and how we can all help create an inclusive classroom and school.

We can help prevent and counter prejudice and racism through anti-bias education.

Anti-bias education

Internationally respected author and anti-bias educator, Louise Derman-Sparks, has advocated anti-bias education in early childhood education throughout her career. Her groundbreaking work is excellent, and I believe it is essential learning and has enormous relevance for teachers of children of all ages.

She and her colleague, Julie Olsen Edwards, have identified four Anti-Bias Education Goals, which are also foundational to developing intercultural understanding.

They are:

Goal One: (*Identity*) Each child will demonstrate self-awareness, confidence, family pride, and positive social/group identities.

Goal Two: (*Diversity*) Each child will express comfort and joy with human diversity, accurate language for human differences, and deep, caring human connections.

Goal Three: (*Justice*) Each child will increasingly recognize unfairness (injustice), have language to describe unfairness, and understand that unfairness hurts.

Goal Four: (*Activism*) Each child will demonstrate a sense of empowerment and the skills to act, with others or alone, against prejudice and/or discriminatory actions.
(Derman-Sparks and Olsen Edwards (2010) in Derman-Sparks and Olsen Edwards (2016)).

Both educators advocate that all four goals be actively addressed for all children, white children and children of colour, every day if anti-bias education is to be effective. All four goals are interdependent and are necessary to help all children develop healthy racial identities. They have found that many teachers bypass goals three and four and are reluctant to talk about race with children because of their own discomfort. They do not feel equipped to do so and are afraid they will make the problem worse. The authors make the point that it is silence in the face of stereotypes and discrimination that results in children learning prejudice.

Stacey York, another advocate and authority on anti-bias education, has done exemplary work in the field of anti-bias early childhood education. I find her seminal work, *Roots and Wings: Affirming Culture and Preventing Bias in Early Childhood* (2016), an exceptional and comprehensive guide to providing culturally relevant anti-bias curriculum. It contains a wealth of activities and ideas to help young children develop into strong, confident young people who embrace difference and stand up to injustice for themselves and others. She models ways we can talk with children about stereotypes and prejudice, and she encourages them to be 'strong and proud' in the ways they respond.

Two other resources you may find useful are the websites for Teaching Tolerance www.tolerance.org, and Welcoming Schools, www.welcomingschools.org. The Teaching Tolerance Anti-Bias Framework K-12 (Teaching Tolerance, 2014) provides excellent resources for teachers. HRC Welcoming Schools program provides excellent resources for teachers and parents to help make our schools safe and inclusive learning environments for children.

Respecting and engaging with difference is not just about differences in race, culture, ethnicity and language. When we respect the human rights and dignity of all others our engagement with difference includes gender, gender identification, LGBTQ, body size and shape, age, socioeconomic status, ability, and physical and learning differences.

Words are very powerful and carry with them underlying meaning. Educators are becoming increasingly aware of the words and terms we use and the unintended effects they often have to reinforce stereotypes and labels. For example, within educational discourse teachers are increasingly replacing the word *disability* with *difference*.

I believe we also need to help children develop compassion and respect for people from different socioeconomic groups. We can help children understand that we are all born into different family and living situations, and regardless of what we have we all have the right to be treated with respect and dignity.

There are beautiful examples of children engaging with difference with kindness and compassion.

There is a lovely video I watched on *The Independent* website (23 May 2017) of seven-year-old school children greeting a classmate who returned to school with her new prosthetic leg. She was met with a heartwarming combination of curiosity, love and inclusion. The children's comments could be heard among the excitement, 'Is that your new pink leg?' 'Wow!' 'It's cool!' and there were hugs, followed by the children running and marching together in the playground.

It is important to remember that love and kindness are also alive and well in our world. Keep your eye out for stories like these to add to your resource files for use with your students.

Exploring and managing our emotions

Children's social and emotional learning is a central part of school curricula and is woven into all that we do. Educators, parents and caregivers have an important role in helping children recognise, express and manage their emotions in healthy ways, which are essential life skills.

Engaging with difference requires confidence and courage, and the ability to manage uncertainty and discomfort. We can help children explore their emotions when faced with difference, and develop positive strategies such as asking questions, being brave, and using mindfulness techniques that help them engage with rather than withdraw from difference. Many schools are now including mindfulness practice in the curriculum to contribute to children's well-being. Mindfulness practice helps children be fully present and aware in the moment, and can be particularly effective in helping them manage their emotions when faced with new and potentially stressful situations. It is also important to help children know that when a situation feels unsafe they should seek the help of a trusted adult.

In the 'Introduction' of this book I told the story of the six-year-old child who knew that engaging with difference requires courage and confidence, when he said that, 'When they hear people talking another language they don't feel scared'.

'Reaching in' and 'reaching out'

The expectation for people to assimilate in their new cities and countries still exists in most places. We often find that groups of people who are new to a place are isolated or marginalised, rather than well-integrated into the new community. This happens in our towns and cities, and in our schools, where different ethnic groups, including immigrants and refugees, often remain separate. This is usually due to fear of difference, prejudice about different cultures or perceived socioeconomic status or language.

In Chapter 5 I discussed the difference between *assimilation* and *integration*, and it is integration that honours our diversity and helps create inclusive communities. For integration to be successful I believe we need to adopt the concepts of 'reaching in' and 'reaching out' where newcomers and established residents assume a shared responsibility to engage with each other. Newcomers to a community have a responsibility to 'reach in' and embrace the new cultures and languages of the place they are moving to while they also retain their own cultures and languages. The community likewise has a responsibility to 'reach out' to the newcomers and embrace the cultures and languages they bring as well.

It is the same when a new child joins a new school. To ensure a successful transition a new child can learn to 'reach in' to the cultures of the class, school and community, and the children of the class can learn to 'reach out' to the new child, welcoming him or her and the cultural, ethnic and linguistic backgrounds he or she brings. This demonstrates the intention on everyone's part to create inclusive communities where everyone feels like they belong. As educators we can model this for our students, and provide opportunities for them to learn about and practise 'reaching in' and 'reaching out' in school and in the community.

This is what it might look like:

Imagine that a Dutch family has just enrolled in your school in London. You and your students would prepare for the new child's arrival. You could make a welcome sign in Dutch and English, learn greetings and basic phrases in Dutch, and create a Dutch/English phrasebook. You might learn a bit about The Netherlands beforehand and create a welcome notice board with photographs of famous Dutch sights paired with famous sights in London. The school would provide a buddy family to help the new family settle in.

The child and his or her parents would ask questions and show interest in learning about the British way of life and be open to trying new things.

We would see:

- People learning greetings and basic phrases in each other's languages, and making an effort to communicate with each other.
- People showing an interest in each other's cultures and customs.
- People inviting each other to join them in social and community events.

You as the teacher can help facilitate a new child's transition. My book, *New Kid in School: Using Literature to Help Children in Transition* (Rader and Sittig, 2003), is a resource specifically dedicated to this topic.

This will be very sensitive when welcoming refugee children who have experienced the pain and trauma of living through conflict and leaving their country. They need to be reassured that you and your class will help them make a new life here. It is a delicate balance to acknowledge their country and culture without triggering painful memories. You can help facilitate this by preparing for the new child's arrival, 'reaching out', and inviting and encouraging the child and his or her family to 'reach in'.

When children do not feel a sense of belonging and connection with those around them it not only affects their learning, but they can more easily become vulnerable and at risk for social and emotional difficulties.

Nelson Mandela wisely said, 'If you talk to a man in a language he understands that goes to his head. If you talk to him in his language, that goes to his heart'. When we are 'reaching in' and 'reaching out' we can begin to speak to each other's hearts.

PAUSE FOR REFLECTION

How could you help your students begin to 'reach in' and 'reach out' in your class and school?

How could you help your students learn to 'reach in' and 'reach out' with others in the local community?

Closing

Once you begin to see life through the lens of intercultural understanding you will find references to it all around you; in the books you read, the films you see, the exhibitions you attend and more. And these will become your examples as you share your observations and insights with your colleagues, students and their families.

I remember reading *H is for Hawk* by Helen Macdonald. While it is a book about grief and hawks it is also a book about life and love. Helen is a keen observer of life, and in her interview with National Public Radio (NPR) in the States she said of Britain, and I believe it is true of many countries in our world, that it's a land of otherness. It's a land of difference and immigrants and complicated relationships that we just don't often see, and one of the things the hawk taught her was to notice those things. What a powerful lesson, to notice difference! And I would take this further and say that we all benefit from learning to notice both the similarities we share and the differences between us.

Hedy Schleifer ends her TEDxTelAviv Talk with this powerful statement. 'I envision a time when nations will know that the space between them is sacred space. That there is a bridge to cross to know the culture of the other and that we can encounter each other human essence to human essence.' Extending her hope for our world, I envision a time when not only nations, but also the people within those nations in our multicultural homes, schools and communities, will cross the bridge to know each other. Teaching and learning for intercultural understanding in our schools can help make that happen.

Concepts featured in the learning engagements

We can learn to anticipate and normalise difference

When we embrace the diverse nature of our world and its people, difference is seen as a natural part of human diversity and to be expected. The more we learn about and interact with different people and cultures the more natural it feels.

We can learn to recognise, challenge and resist stereotypes and prejudice

Stereotypes and prejudice are learned behaviours. As we develop awareness and a belief in equity and human rights, we can challenge what we see and hear. We can help children see how recognising and challenging stereotypes, and standing up to prejudice and discrimination protects the well-being, rights and dignity of others.

Courage and confidence to engage with difference exists within each one of us

Each one of us has the capacity to dig deep and tap into our inner confidence and courage. As educators we must find the confidence and courage within ourselves and create opportunities for children to recognise and develop it in themselves.

Both 'reaching in' and 'reaching out' are necessary for effective integration

When individuals 'reach in' and 'reach out' there is intention on the part of both newcomers and established residents to honour each other's differences, and develop relationships and communities where everyone feels like they belong. 'Reaching in' and 'reaching out' creates a sense of belonging and connection for everyone. It establishes trust and goodwill between diverse people.

Reflection is an essential skill for intercultural understanding

When we carefully consider our actions and reactions, and those of others, we gain personal and cultural awareness and knowledge which leads to greater intercultural understanding. This in turn guides our behaviour in important ways. We can model and provide opportunities for children to learn and practise reflection as a valuable life skill.

Multicultural friendships and relationships enlarge our world and enrich our lives

Children benefit from friendships with children of other cultures in many ways. They learn new ways of doings things, try different foods, share in each other's celebrations, learn each other's language, play each other's games and listen to each other's music. Some of these new experiences may even become part of their daily lives.

(Rader and Sittig, 2003)

Learning outcomes

Learners will:

- Begin to learn about stereotypes, prejudice, discrimination and racism, and their impact.
- Develop the ability to recognise, challenge and resist stereotypes, prejudice, discrimination and racism.
- Begin to reflect on intercultural experiences, and anticipate and understand that differences exist.
- Become willing and able to modify their thinking and behaviour when their experience differs from their assumptions and expectations.
- Seek commonalities, and learn about 'reaching in' and 'reaching out'.
- Develop and practise skills for peaceful conflict resolution and mediation.
- Begin to develop a range of socially and culturally appropriate behaviour according to the situation or context.
- Explore the emotions associated with change, discomfort and uncertainty, and healthy ways to address them.
- Begin to develop self-monitoring and self-management skills.
- Engage with others who are different from themselves and begin to develop multicultural relationships.

References

Cushner, K, McClelland, A and Safford, P (2015) *Human Diversity in Education: An Intercultural Approach* 8th edition. New York, NY: McGraw Hill Education.

Derman-Sparks, L and Olsen Edwards, J (2010) *Anti-bias Education for Young Children and Ourselves*. Washington, DC: NAEYC.

Derman-Sparks, L and Olsen Edwards, J (2016) *The Goals of Anti-Bias Education Clearing up Some Key Misconceptions*. www.antibiasleadersece.com/wp-content/uploads/2016/07/Goals-of-ABEMisconceptions.pdf

Holladay, J R (2000) *White Anti-Racist Activism: A Personal Roadmap*. Roselle, NJ: Crandall, Dostie & Douglass Books, Inc. www.tolerance.org/professional-development/on-racism-and-white-privilege

Lieff, J M.D. Blog (October 2014): http://jonlieffmd.com/blog/prejudice-stereotypes-reside-brain (accessed January 2018).

Luu, Chi (2017) 'Does Your Accent Make You Smarter?': www.bbc.com/capital/story/20170523-does-your-accent-make-you-sound-smarter (accessed January 2018).

MacDonald, H interview with NPR (2015) on *H is for Hawk*.

No Bully: www.nobully.org

Rader, D and Sittig, L (2003) *New Kid in School: Using Literature to Help Children in Transition*. New York, NY: Teachers College Press.

Schleifer, H (2010) 'The Power of Connection'. TEDxTelAviv Talk April 2010.

The Independent: www.independent.co.uk/news/uk/home-news/seven-year-old-girl-anu-activity-prosthetic-blade-best-reaction-friends-birmingham-a7716046.html (accessed May 2017).

Teaching Tolerance (2014) *The Teaching Tolerance Anti-Bias Framework K-12*. Montgomery, AL: Southern Poverty Law Center. www.tolerance.org/sites/default/files/general/TT%20anti%20bias%20framework%20pamphlet_final.pdf

Tolerance.org: www.tolerance.org

Welcoming Schools: www.welcomingschools.org

York, S (2016) *Roots and Wing: Affirming Culture and Preventing Bias in Early Childhood*. St Paul MN: Redleaf Press.

Lesson plan: Reception–Year 6

Amazing Grace

by Mary Hoffman
Illustrated by Caroline Binch

Synopsis

I have loved this book ever since it was first published in 1991. Grace loves stories, all kinds of stories. She has a wonderful imagination and loves acting out the most exciting parts. One day her teacher tells the class they will put on the play *Peter Pan*. Grace along with many of her classmates wants to be Peter, but other children tell her she can't be Peter Pan because she is a girl and because she is black. Grace's mother and grandmother support and encourage her to follow her desire regardless of what others say, which she does. With courage and determination she brings her talent and skill to the role, and Grace, quite simply is amazing!

This story provides an excellent springboard for children to learn about and discuss stereotypes, prejudice, discrimination and racism, and their impact. You can use this book to explore ways to recognise, challenge and resist them, speak out and take action, and see how we can modify our thinking and behaviour when we learn that our assumptions are inaccurate.

These are suggested definitions of the terms for children:

> *Stereotype*: A general way of thinking about a group of people that is unfair and untrue.
>
> *Prejudice*: Opinion about a person or group based on stereotypes that is usually negative.
>
> *Discrimination*: Actions based on prejudice.
>
> *Racism*: When people in power use prejudice against other people or groups.

Learning outcomes

Learners will:

- Begin to learn about and understand stereotypes, prejudice, discrimination and racism and the ways they affect others.
- Develop the ability to recognise, challenge and resist stereotypes, prejudice, discrimination and racism.
- Begin to see how we can change our thinking and behaviour when our experience differs from our assumptions or expectations.
- Begin to stand up to injustice, and speak out and take action.

Pre-reading activities

- Explore the concept of stereotypes with your students. Begin with a conversation about gender stereotypes and the ideas that some people have about boys and girls. Choose several

One Green Apple

by Eve Bunting
Illustrated by Ted Lewin

Synopsis

This is the story of a young Muslim girl called Farah who moves to the United States. It is her second day of school and the class is taking a trip to an apple orchard. She does not speak English yet, and feels alone and lost in the new place. When the children pick apples to make apple cider she chooses a green apple, unlike the red apples her classmates choose, which shows how different she feels. This story helps develop empathy for what it is like for immigrant children coming to a new country. It is a story about assimilation, and provides an opportunity to learn the difference between assimilation and integration. It lends itself particularly well to teaching children the difference between 'belonging' and 'fitting in', and the concepts of 'reaching in' and 'reaching out'. It can be used effectively to learn about stereotypes and prejudice some people have about people who are different, and how and why these develop. This story also develops empathy for all others who move to a new place.

You can paraphrase the story for young children and choose the learning engagements that are most appropriate.

Learning outcomes

Learners will:

- Begin to learn about stereotypes and prejudice, and their impact on others.
- Develop the ability to recognise, challenge and resist stereotypes and prejudice.
- Begin to reflect on intercultural experiences, and anticipate and understand that differences exist.
- Seek commonalities, and learn about 'reaching in' and 'reaching out'.
- Begin to develop a range of culturally and socially appropriate behaviour according to the situation or context.
- Explore the emotions associated with change, discomfort and uncertainty, and healthy ways to address them.
- Engage with others who are different from themselves and begin to develop multicultural relationships.

Pre-reading activities

- Begin a discussion about what it is like to be new in a new place. Draw on your students' own experiences of mobility, and the experiences of their family, friends or neighbours who may have moved. Identify the challenges that children and adults may face, including not knowing the language, and the feelings they may have. Extend the discussion to talk about the additional challenges for immigrants and refugees.

- It is helpful to define these terms with children:

  Immigrant: a person who moves to another country, usually permanently.

  Refugee: a person who flees to another country for safety or protection from trouble or danger.

  Migrant: a person who moves to another country or region, usually temporarily.

- Introduce the book, and discuss the picture on the cover and what the story might be about. The children will notice Farah is wearing a dupatta, or headscarf, and that she is holding a green apple while the other children are picking red ones. Discuss possible reasons why and tell them to listen to find out.

Post-reading activities

- Explain that Farah is Muslim and that some, however not all, Muslim girls and women wear a dupatta to cover their hair for religious reasons, or as part of their cultural identity or for fashion.

  This is a good opportunity to explain the difference in headscarves from the notes at the end of the lesson plan. You may wish to show your students photographs of the salwar kameez and dupatta, the sari and the hijab. Tell the children that we do not know what country Farah's family is from and what language(s) they speak. Explain that we cannot make assumptions about where a person is from or their beliefs based on what they wear or what they look like. We must be willing to engage with them and get to know them to know their story.

- Revisit the text and illustrations, and discuss the following questions:

  How does Farah feel in her new country and school and why? Possible answers may be she feels lonely and alone because she does not understand the language, different because she is the only one wearing a headscarf and it may also be uncomfortable for her to have boys and girls sit together which they do not do in her home country.

  Farah thinks, 'It's odd to have boys and girls sit together.' Explain that it is uncommon for boys and girls to sit together in Muslim countries. How did Farah manage her discomfort? She had confidence and courage, recognised and accepted things were different, and was open to new ways of doing things. Explain that some children switch languages and adapt their behaviour when they are at school and when they are at home. Acknowledge the experiences of your students for whom this may also be true.

  Have you ever been in a situation where someone else had religious traditions that were different from yours? How did you feel? How did you respond to the situation? Discuss how we can hold on to our own beliefs without being threatened by others, and be open to learning about theirs. What do we need to do so? (be curious, interested, accepting, tolerant).

  What are some of the challenges Farah faced? Possible answers might be she left her country and dog behind, the customs are different, some people have a negative view about her country and culture, and she doesn't speak the language of her new country.

- Look at the expressions on the children's faces on the hay wagon. Why do some children look at Farah 'coldly and smile cruel smiles', and 'mention her country in a negative way'? They may have stereotypes and prejudice, and judge all Muslims to be a certain way. Discuss reasons stereotypes are wrong. Establish that they are not true about everyone, are unfair and hurtful, they keep us from knowing people and understanding them, they can limit other people and keep them from being all they can be, and they can affect the way people interact with them

Lesson plan: Reception–Year 6

The Other Side

by Jacqueline Woodson
Illustrations by E B Lewis

Synopsis

This is a beautiful book to begin to address prejudice and racism, and how it can be overcome. Clover and Annie live on separate sides of the fence that segregates the black side of town and the white side. That summer they find a way to develop a friendship despite the fence between them. This book inspires hope that we, too, can overcome the 'fences' that exist in our lives and world.

Learning outcomes

Learners will:

- Begin to learn about stereotypes, prejudice, discrimination and racism, and their impact.
- Develop the ability to recognise, challenge and resist stereotypes, prejudice, discrimination and racism.
- Begin to stand up to injustice, and speak out and take action.
- Become willing and able to modify their thinking and behaviour when their experience differs from their assumptions and expectations.
- Seek commonalities and learn about 'reaching out' to others.
- Become more observant and reflect on what they notice (see Chapter 8).
- Explore the emotions associated with discomfort and uncertainty, and healthy ways to address them.
- Engage with others who are different from themselves and begin to develop multicultural relationships.

Pre-reading activities

- Introduce the title and cover of the book, and invite any questions, wonderings, predictions and observations about the story. The children will notice that Clover, the black girl, is in the foreground, and that a fence separates her and Annie, a white girl, on the other side. Discuss why this might be. The story is told from Clover's point of view, and this is a story that takes place in a time when black and white people were legally segregated.

This story presents an opportunity for children to learn about segregation. Check for background knowledge. Explain that in the past it was legal in some states in the United States to discriminate against black people. Laws were passed that separated where blacks and whites lived and went to school, the drinking fountains and toilets they used, where they sat on the bus, and more. Some people had mistaken thinking and thought African American people were not equal to white people. Some people still think that today even though the Civil Rights Act was passed in 1964 to end discrimination. We know this is not true, and that everyone is important and has value, and people continue to fight for equal treatment for everyone today. We also know that people with skin of different colours are and can be our friends.

Affirm the multicultural and multiracial friendships you and the children have in your classroom and school. They may be with other children, teachers, bus drivers, after-school club leaders and others.

Tell the children this story is about two girls, Clover and Annie, who find a way to reach out and become friends even though their lives are separated by the fence.

Discuss the following questions. Why are the girls staring at each other? (maybe they want to be friends, maybe they are curious about each other). What might the girls be thinking? Possible answers might be 'I wonder who she is.' 'I wonder what she is like.' 'I wish I could play with her on that tyre swing.' Have you ever wondered what someone you didn't know was like? What about someone who was different from you?

Post-reading activities

- Invite the children to share their responses to the story.

  Lead a rich discussion and explore the following questions.

- How did Clover and Annie become friends? Both girls first watched each other over a period of time. Discuss how we can learn about other people by observing them. Emphasise the point that taking the time to notice things can help us learn more about people and places. What do you think they learned about each other? (Clover probably noticed Annie was lonely and would like a friend, and that she seemed playful splashing in the puddles and was friendly. Annie probably saw a possible friend, and that Clover seemed kind and was curious about her, too.) Ask, What have you observed about another person before becoming friends with him or her?

  Annie was friendly, brave and outgoing and asked the girls if she could play. When Sandra said no she didn't give up and continued to sit on the fence. When Clover came near the fence Annie took the first step to reach out and asked Clover her name. Clover responded, and they both exchanged smiles of friendship. Discuss how 'reaching out' and responding to someone's gesture of friendship are both necessary to start a relationship. Invite the children to tell about a time they became friends with someone who is different from them.

- Ask your students to imagine a conversation between Annie and Clover. What do you think they talked about that summer? In pairs have your students act out a conversation they might have had. It might be about finding things they have in common or why their mothers thought it was unsafe to play together, or why there was this silly fence and their hope for the future. Your students will have many creative and insightful ideas!

- What would you have done if you were Clover or Annie? Some children may say they would not be friends because she is black or white. Use this as an opportunity to address fear of difference and correct mistaken thinking. Talk about how everyone has different coloured skin and could be a friend. Lead these discussions with compassion and understanding, and use this as an opportunity for teaching and raising self-awareness. Help children to think deeply about where their ideas came from. You might say, 'I wonder why you think this.' or ask the question, 'Where do you think this idea came from?'

- What did Clover and Annie teach the other children? Possible answers might be to resist your fear, stereotypes, prejudice and discrimination, to not let the colour of a person's skin keep you from getting to know him or her, to question things you think are not right, and to stand up and take action for what you believe. Invite the children to share a time they stood up for what they knew was right. What qualities were needed? How could you develop them?

Beginning to assume responsibility for making a positive difference in our world is addressed in the discussions and activities identifying and removing invisible fences that exist.

Chapter 8: 'Developing essential intercultural, interpersonal and life skills'

Learners will:
Develop increased problem-solving and decision-making skills.
Consider and develop multiple perspectives.
Develop increased creative and critical thinking skills.

- Annie had another perspective about the fence and said, 'A fence like this was meant for sitting on'. She thought the fence did not have to separate them but could bring them together. Clover listened to her point of view and chose to join her. Both girls were independent thinkers and questioned what adults had said. Ask: Have you ever questioned rules that seemed unfair?

- Clover and Annie found a way to obey their parents and also be friends. They also developed a friendship even though Sandra and Clover's other friends disagreed with Clover. Discuss how the two girls were creative and independent thinkers. They questioned what they had heard and thought was not right. They reached out to each other and through their experience they learned that they could be friends with someone of a different race.

  Discuss in small groups, How can you be an independent thinker when your parents and friends hold a different view? Have your students create a *Guide to Becoming an Independent Thinker*. This could be the basis for a school-wide publication or assembly, and shared with the school community.

- Have your students consider different perspectives. Have them write a conversation between Clover's mother and Annie's mother, between Annie and her mother, or between Clover and her mother about the fence and their hope for the future. Share the conversations.

  Explore different perspectives further as you discuss the differences that exist in the ways families do things, the ideas they have and the way they live their lives. Clover's mother did not want her to play in the rain while Annie could. Why? What are some ways your family may be different from someone else's? Discuss how we can understand and accept cultural perspectives that may be different from our own.

Chapter 9: 'Embedding local and global issues'

Learners will:
Begin to develop personal and social responsibility for addressing racism locally and globally.

- Racism is a significant local and global issue in many parts of the world. Provide ways for your students to engage in projects within the school that educate others about racism and ways they can stand up to racism. Learn about social action projects online that your students might participate in.

Notes

Introduce or review the meaning of the terms *stereotype, prejudice, discrimination* and *racism* suggested in the lesson plan for *Amazing Grace*.

When addressing the topics of stereotypes, prejudice, discrimination and racism some children may express beliefs that are hurtful or offensive. It is important to acknowledge children's comments, to ask questions to understand children's thinking and to respond in a non-evaluative way. Our aim is to facilitate learning and to raise self-awareness.

I was first introduced to using a heart-shaped cushion at a clowning workshop I attended where the cushion was passed round as we introduced ourselves to the group. It served many purposes from giving us a physical object to help us connect to our heart space, to easing anxiety for some of the participants. I thought I had to have one for working with children and find it a helpful tool to use when discussing important topics. Sometimes it is placed in the middle of the circle or sits nearby, but it is always with us. Consider the ways you might use one – or a similar object – as well. It is used in this lesson as you explore the concept of hope.

8

Developing essential intercultural, interpersonal and life skills

Introduction

Overview

We share our planet with a wonderfully diverse group of human beings with whom we live, love, learn, work, create and play. They are our families, friends, neighbours, teachers, classmates, colleagues, shopkeepers, doctors, librarians and many, many others. And we interact with people of different races, cultures, languages and faiths on a daily basis. Intercultural, interpersonal and life skills are essential for developing and maintaining healthy and positive human relationships within and across cultures. If we are to work towards our vision for a better world it is vital that we develop skills that help us understand each other, show respect for each other, and have empathy for and help each other. It is essential that we help children develop the same. I believe we need to intentionally teach for human relationships and help make relational learning visible for children.

Effective communication is at the heart of healthy relationships. I am writing from a Western Anglo–American perspective. However, effective communication may look, sound and feel different in other cultures. The important point is that we acknowledge that differences exist, be willing to recognise and accept other styles of communication and different views, and use our skills, and adapt our words and behaviour as needed to communicate effectively and appropriately.

What does it look like when people communicate respectfully and effectively? What might we see people doing?

People may appear calm, lean in, nod in some way to let the other person know they are listening, and make appropriate eye contact. We may see people take turns, speak without interrupting and encourage everyone's participation.

What does it sound like? What might we hear people saying?

We might hear people rephrase what the other person has said, ask questions to learn, understand and clarify what has been said, and build on and respond to each other's ideas. They may make suggestions for compromise, and seek and negotiate fair outcomes.

People may invite dialogue through phrases such as, 'Tell me about. . .' or 'Can you explain. . .?'. They might expand the conversation with phrases such as 'I wonder if. . .', 'What do you think about. . . ?' or 'Tell me more about. . .'. They may check for understanding and paraphrase using words such as, 'It sounds like. . .' or 'So you think. . . ?' They might think, 'Does he/she understand me?' 'How can I say this differently?'

What does it feel like on the inside?

People may feel calm, fully present, connected, acknowledged and heard, and therefore trusting and open to making connections.

These skills help us to thrive in our families, schools, communities and the wider world. We as educators are most effective when we model these skills, provide opportunities for children to learn and practise them, and recognise and reinforce these skills when we see children acquire and use them.

We could consider the following as essential life skills. They overlap dynamically. They help us navigate and adapt in a multicultural, connected world where constant change is the norm.

Intercultural skills

Intercultural skills include *intercultural awareness, intercultural sensitivity* and *intercultural communication.*

Intercultural awareness is understanding our own and other cultures, and the similarities and differences between them. It is knowing that similarities and differences exist between and within cultures. It begins with an awareness of one's own cultures, beliefs, values and attitudes. It is knowing that others may do and see things differently than we do.

Intercultural awareness is often paired with *intercultural sensitivity,* which is the understanding that other people's cultures and languages are important to them in the way ours are to us, and therefore should be respected. We are therefore willing and able to adapt our words and behaviour in different situations, and make sure the language we use is inclusive and does not cause offence. Chen and Starosta (1997) describe intercultural sensitivity as, 'an individual's ability to develop emotion towards understanding and appreciating cultural differences that promotes appropriate and effective behaviour in intercultural communication'.

Intercultural communication is the way people communicate between different cultural and language groups. Intercultural communication requires knowledge about other cultures and skills to interact effectively with people from different cultures. It requires empathy and the ability to see things from another person's perspective, as well as the ability to adapt our language and behaviour. Intercultural communication is both verbal and non-verbal, and we can learn important information about cultural differences by listening to and watching others. Barrett (2016) identifies active listening and observing as the skills required to notice and understand what is being said and how it is being said, and to notice and understand other people's non-verbal behaviour. This includes differences such as gestures, facial expressions, tone of voice, patterns of speech and eye movement.

I included a lesson plan for *Marianthe's Story: Painted Words and Spoken Memories* in *New Kid in School* (Rader and Sittig, 2003), and also in this chapter. In the story, Mari's mother suggests that she *look, listen and learn* to adjust to her new country, culture and school. This is an excellent approach to transition, and also to learning about other cultures. I have added the first step, STOP, to encourage children to wait to respond and not react. I have found that a simple way to help children begin to develop intercultural skills is by encouraging them to STOP, LOOK, LISTEN and LEARN.

STOP: Wait before we judge a situation, make assumptions and respond.

LOOK: Observe people, places and situations.

LISTEN: Listen to what people say and how they say it, and try to understand their intended message.

LEARN: Ask questions to gain information, clarify our perceptions and then communicate with understanding.

It is also important to develop intercultural skills as children engage in learning in virtual environments and on social media platforms. Intercultural skills are usually addressed in digital citizenship programmes in schools, and are essential skills for children and adults in our highly technological world.

Interpersonal skills

There are many interpersonal skills that are important to develop for effective living. Communication is one of the most important. Children need to be able to articulate their thoughts and ideas effectively and listen and respond to those of others. Here I focus on the communication skills of listening, questioning, observing and responding.

Listening and questioning

Listening is perhaps the most important skill we can develop for healthy intercultural and interpersonal relationships. Good listening builds positive relationships, and is critical to problem-solving and conflict resolution. We need to explicitly teach listening skills, and emphasise our intention to understand the other person's ideas, needs and feelings. We can ask the person to slow down or please repeat something we have not heard properly. We can teach children reflective listening and help children develop the vocabulary for reflective listening starting with phrases or questions such as, 'It sounds like. . .' or 'So you feel. . . ?'. Most importantly we need to provide opportunities for children to practise good listening skills.

One of the most useful communication strategies I learned was from William Powell, in his Leadership and Group Dynamics course at the Principals' Training Centre (PTC). He called it the 'power of the pause' and it is essentially wait time to give the person you are communicating with time to respond. It also lets the other person know you are listening as you take time to consider your response. Some classroom teachers are teaching pausing to their students as part of effective listening skills and you may wish to as well.

Listening skills are easier to use when we agree with the other person. What is important is to help children learn to listen to those with whom they disagree. Many people identify strongly with their beliefs, and seem to have a need to be right and hold on to them tightly. When we are confident in who we are, we are more willing to see different perspectives as equally valid.

Many of us are finding that our family and friends hold views that are surprisingly contrary to what we thought and to the ones we hold. Listening and understanding different points of view are essential if we are to stay connected and engage in conversation. During recent election campaigns in the US and UK I, like many, read widely and talked with others, wanting to understand what people with different political views felt strongly about and why. There is a tendency to disregard people and topics we do not agree with rather than seek understanding and common ground. These are important skills for adults to develop so that we can help children engage in conversation and learn to be open to other perspectives from an early age.

When we ask questions with a genuine desire to learn and understand we show our interest and intention to connect with others. This sometimes requires humility and our willingness to admit that we do not know. Both listening and questioning are essential to facilitate effective communication.

Observing and responding

We can gain important cultural and personal knowledge by observing others if we do so with the intention of learning and understanding. We can learn appropriate ways of behaving in different social settings and cultural contexts. I love the way Rana DiOrio, author of the *What Does It Mean to Be. . .?*® series of children's books, describes some of her own intercultural skills. In her bibliography on her author's page, she says, 'I believe that I have two ears, two eyes and one mouth intentionally so I listen and observe more than I talk. As a result, I think I am better able to respect and appreciate diversity.' This is a lovely anecdote to share and discuss with children as we begin to teach intercultural communication skills.

The way that we respond to others is also critical to effective and appropriate communication. We can help children see the impact of their verbal and non-verbal behaviour and understand the importance of communicating with respect. This is reflected in behaviours such as our tone of voice, the words we choose and our body language. It includes humility and apologising if we have offended someone. There may be instances where we may need to politely explain that something someone has done is done differently, or considered rude or offensive in our culture.

PAUSE FOR REFLECTION

How do you help your students see things from different perspectives?

How do you help develop intercultural awareness, intercultural sensitivity and intercultural communication skills in your students?

How do you develop effective listening, questioning, observing and responding skills in your students? How could you integrate them more explicitly?

Conflict resolution

Our world has seen an increasing climate of insults and anger, which makes it even more important to teach children to maintain their integrity, communicate respectfully, and realise that we control our behaviour and the ways in which we respond. When conflicts arise we can learn to ask questions respectfully, listen carefully and non-judgementally with the intention of understanding, and respond tactfully. We may find that we hold similar values, yet have a different way of expressing them. The idea that others can also be right is at the heart of intercultural understanding. As we discussed in Chapter 7 we need to enter into dialogue with others with the intention of understanding each other's perspectives so we can build consensus, compromise and find fair solutions.

Life skills

The following are additional life skills that particularly contribute to the disposition and competence of intercultural understanding.

We provide opportunities for children to develop *creative and critical thinking, problem-solving and decision-making,* and *collaboration and cooperation* in our schools every day. It is helpful if you model these skills and share with your students the ways you use them in your own life.

Creative and critical thinking

Creative thinking is the ability to look at a problem or situation in different ways. This could involve seeing a different way to do something, generating new ideas, or using materials in unique ways. Creative thinkers experiment, take risks and are willing to make mistakes. Critical thinking skills involve analysing, synthesising, conceptualising, applying and evaluating information.

Problem-solving and decision-making

We all solve problems and make decisions in every aspect of our lives every day, and we apply creative and critical thinking skills to do so. We identify the problem, generate possible solutions, evaluate them and decide on one. If the first approach is not effective we try another. When making decisions we identify and evaluate the pros and cons, and consider the outcome and the effect of the decision on the people involved.

Collaboration and cooperation

Collaboration and cooperation are both equally important skills. Collaboration is working together as a team and sharing ideas to solve a problem, and involves compromise and consensus. Cooperation involves distinct roles where individual skills and abilities are aligned and used to solve the problem.

It is helpful to talk with your students about different ways we can show leadership as we collaborate and cooperate. We might bring people together for a common cause or lead by example. Encourage them to lead when they can and be a supportive follower when it is appropriate, too, as they collaborate and support others' initiatives.

Building resilience and managing change

Building resilience is a necessary prerequisite for managing change effectively. Resilience involves confidence, adaptability and determination, and believing we have the ability to manage challenging situations when they arise. I think of resilience as character traits reinforced by a sense of connectedness and community, and where we can ask for help if we need it. This is illustrated by the examples below, which also reflect cultural differences.

Geoff Smith, Head Teacher at Kehelland Village School in Cornwall, illustrates the way intentional teaching about character traits can build resilience. Teachers invoke the virtues children learn through The Virtues Project by embedding them in real-life experiences. For example, each term the children embark on a trek to develop resilience.

Before departing, the children are asked to name the virtues they will need on the journey such as patience, determination and courage. Then they are asked to describe how they will call on these virtues. Responses have been, 'We will need to practise patience – it will take some time to reach our journey's end.' and 'We might need to use determination to complete the trek when we feel like giving up!'. On the journey teachers use the language of virtues to guide the children such as, 'What virtue do you need to call on to overcome your fear?' or 'I can see your determination to finish this trek!'. At the end of the journey the children, in dialogue with their peers and class teacher, reflect on the virtues that they used on their journey.

Catherine Panter-Brick, an anthropologist at Yale University, and her colleagues found that young Syrian refugees now living in Jordan said that their resilience came from developing friendships, and their ability to integrate into their new communities. Panter-Brick says that, 'In the West, we tend to think of resilience as inner psychological strength. In the Middle East, resilience is more of a collective and social strength' (Singh, 2017).

It is important to explicitly teach children effective strategies for managing change.

Approaches to transition are embedded in *New Kid in School: Using Literature to Help Children in Transition* (Rader and Sittig, 2003). They include asking questions, planning ahead, being curious, patient and flexible, taking risks and observing differences.

Reflective practice

It is helpful to cultivate reflective practice in children and ourselves so we learn from our experiences. We can help children think about what they did, what happened, what they learned and what they might do differently or the same the next time they encounter a similar situation. Reflection can be as simple as a student's learning log or personal blog, and it should be built into regular practice.

Develop and sustain positive relationships

Developing and sustaining friendships and relationships is an important life skill. In *New Kid in School* (Rader and Sittig, 2003), I dedicated a chapter to 'Friendships and Relationships', which you may find useful as you develop these skills with your students. These interpersonal skills do not always come naturally to children and need to be taught and practised. It is important to be intentional in developing friendships and relationships that embrace people from many cultures.

Mindfulness

'Mindfulness is our ability to be aware of what is going on both inside and around us' (Thich Nhat Hanh, 2008). It focuses on our breathing and being fully present in the moment. Mindfulness practice has been shown to improve attention, executive function, reduce stress, help regulate emotions and increase compassion and empathy leading to greater wellbeing. (Rechtschaffen, 2014). Many teachers are practising mindfulness themselves and schools are integrating mindfulness practice into the school curricula. It is a valuable practice for children and adults.

I was privileged to attend a three-day Educator's Retreat, 'An Exploration of Mindfulness in Education, Developing Compassion and Mindfulness in Children', with Zen Master Thich Nhat Hanh and the monks from Plum Village, held at the American School in London in 2012. It was there that I recognised the value of mindfulness practice with children. These are resources that colleagues and I have found useful and I hope you will, too.

A Handful of Quiet: Happiness in Four Pebbles by Thich Nhat Hanh.

Planting Seeds: Practicing Mindfulness with Children by Thich Nhat Hanh and the Plum Village Community.

Mindful Movements: Ten Exercises for Well-Being by Thich Nhat Hanh.

Sitting Still Like a Frog: Mindfulness Exercises for Kids (and Their Parents) by Eline Snel.

Living our lives with intercultural understanding requires us to be fully present in the moment and mindfulness practice can help support our work in this area in profound ways.

PAUSE FOR REFLECTION

How do you help your students develop these life skills?

How could you help them use these skills more intentionally and routinely?

Concepts featured in the learning engagements

Effective intercultural, interpersonal and life skills are essential in our diverse societies

We interact with people from diverse cultures and who speak different languages on a daily basis. We can help children see the importance of developing intercultural skills to get along with those who are different than they are, and also to understand how these skills are central to positive human relationships with anyone.

There is more than one valid perspective

The idea that there is more than way to look at things is central to intercultural understanding. We can help children develop the awareness that there are multiple perspectives and begin to help develop them.

Listening, questioning, observing and responding are important life skills that can be learned

These communication skills are essential for living and working together in diverse communities and need to be modelled, taught and practised. Children can begin to learn them at an early age.

Collaboration can lead to stronger outcomes and more creative solutions

Each of us brings our unique ideas, life experiences and cultural perspectives to our work together. We can arrive at more creative solutions with richer outcomes when diverse groups work together.

Learning outcomes

Learners will:

- Develop greater intercultural awareness and sensitivity.
- Develop effective communication skills (verbal and non-verbal).
- Become more observant and reflect on what they notice.
- Consider and develop multiple perspectives.
- Explore positive strategies to build resilience and manage change.
- Develop increased creative and critical thinking skills.
- Develop increased problem-solving and decision-making skills.
- Begin to develop skills for effective collaboration and cooperation.
- Develop and sustain positive relationships.

References

Barrett (2016) *Competences for Democratic Culture: Living Together as Equals in Culturally Diverse Societies*. Strasbourg: Council of Europe Publishing.

Chen and Starosta (1997) In X Dai and G-M Chen (2014) *Intercultural Communication Competence: Conceptualization and its Development in Cultural Contexts and Interactions*. Newcastle-upon-Tyne: Cambridge Scholars Publishing.

DiOrio, R: www.amazon.com/Rana-DiOrio/e/B002RMH0KW/refdp_byline_cont_book_1

Nhat Hanh, T (2012) *A Handful of Quiet: Happiness in Four Pebbles*. Berkeley, CA: Plum Blossom Books.

Nhat Hanh, T (2008) *Mindful Movements: Ten Exercises for Well-Being*. Berkeley, CA: Parallax Press.

Nhat Hanh, T and the Plum Village Community (2011) *Planting Seeds: Practicing Mindfulness with Children*. Berkeley, CA: Parallax Press.

Rader, D and Sittig, L (2003) *New Kid in School: Using Literature to Help Children in Transition*. New York, NY: Teachers College Press.

Rechtschaffen, D (2014) *The Way of Mindful Education: Cultivating Well-Being in Teachers and Students*. New York, NY: WW Norton & Company, Inc.

Singh, M (2017) 'How do Refugee Teens Build Resilience?': www.npr.org/sections/goatsandsoda/2017/07/30/540002667/how-do-refugee-teens-build-resilience (accessed July 2017).

Snel, E (2013) *Sitting Still Like a Frog: Mindfulness Exercises for Kids (and Their Parents)*. Boston, MA: Shambala.

childhood friends as models for the characters. Almost every picture book she has designed and written has been autobiographical.

■ Ask your students to listen closely and study the illustrations as you read *Chicken Sunday*. Ask them to see if they can find any details in the book that might have actually come from Ms Polacco's childhood.

Post-reading activities

■ Use the following list to discuss the details in the book which really did come from Ms Polacco's life.

Stewart and Winston Washington really were her best friends.

Miss Eula Mae Washington was the boys' grandmother.

Patricia did go to Miss Eula Mae's house for Sunday dinners.

Patricia taught Winston and Stewart how to make pysanky eggs.

The children did get wrongly accused of vandalising the hat shop.

The children did go to talk to Mr Kodinski, and then were allowed to sell their decorated eggs in his shop.

Mr Kodinski did give them the Easter hat for Miss Eula Mae.

The photographs on the page with Miss Eula Mae and the children having Sunday dinner are the real photographs of Miss Eula Mae's family.

The illustration of Mr Kodinski having tea with the children shows a number tattooed on his arm, indicating that he was a Holocaust survivor.

■ Discuss how Patricia, Winston and Stewart went about trying to solve their dilemma about buying Miss Eula Mae the hat. What were the steps that led to their successful resolution?

They worked cooperatively as a group.

First they assessed the situation and counted the money they had already saved.

They thought of a solution and decided to ask Mr Kodinski for jobs.

They saw the vandalism incident from Mr Kodinski's perspective.

They found a way to resolve their conflict with him.

They used clear communication to state their needs and ask for a job.

They found a fair solution.

■ Discuss the reasons the children were successful with Mr Kodinski. What communication skills did they use that helped them both resolve the conflict and solve the problem? (They looked at the situation from Mr Kodinski's perspective, they told him the truth, they listened to his side of the story, they were open-minded about new ideas, and they found a solution both sides could agree on.) You and your students could draft a list of similar steps for effective communication that could be used in your classroom whenever a conflict arises that needs to be resolved. Point out that the children stood up for themselves and told the truth, but also took action to make things right with Mr Kodinski. It took courage to go to see him but it was the right thing to do. Mr Kodinski called their courage *chutzpah* which is a Yiddish word meaning courage.

■ The painted eggs were a 'peace offering' to Mr Kodinski. Discuss with your students that some-times you can give a small gift as part of resolving a conflict with someone. Explain that rather

149

than a purchased gift, it could be something you made, or a kind note or card. It could simply be the offer of a handshake of friendship.

■ Discuss the ways the children in the story develop intercultural awareness and intercultural communication skills. In the beginning of the story, Winnie is fearful about approaching Mr Kodinski for work as he says he is strange, never smiles, and looks mean. After spending an afternoon talking together, having tea and cake, and telling each other about their lives, the children and Mr Kodinski get to know each other. What do you think the children and Mr Kodinski learned about each other? In what ways might the children now have a better understanding of Mr Kodinski and his life? Discuss the approaches they used. (They took time to listen and were open to learning about each other.) Discuss ways people can address their fears when they meet people who are different. Suggestions might include being open to learning about their culture and themselves as individuals, and refraining from judgement.

Suggested follow-up activities

■ The title of this book is very appropriate because the special relationship that Ms Polacco had with Miss Eula Mae centered on the experience of having Sunday dinners at Miss Eula Mae's home. The fact that Miss Eula Mae always served a special meal of fried chicken, collard greens and fried spoon bread led Patricia Polacco to think of those occasions as 'Chicken Sundays'. Ask your students to think of a traditional meal that they have when visiting relatives, or friends, or that someone in their own home prepares for special occasions. Ask them to write a journal entry describing that meal, the occasion and the people involved. You may want to model this first with a memory from your own life. Invite each child to read his or her piece to a classmate, or share it with the entire class.

■ Apologising for something is one of the hardest things for people of all ages to do. Have your students write role-play scenarios involving a conflict with someone where they hurt the other person's feelings or did something wrong. A true apology involves more than just saying, 'I'm sorry'. Ask them to carefully think through the conversation they would have. Have each student read his or her scenario and choose other classmates to play the other parts. Have the students act them out for the rest of the class and discuss them. Include scenarios where there is a cultural misunderstanding and how that is resolved.

Links with learning outcomes in other chapters

This book links with learning outcomes in the following chapters:

Chapter 4: 'Exploring culture and language'

Learners will:
Gain knowledge and appreciation of their own cultures and languages, and those of others, and develop an interest in learning about them.
Gain knowledge of different cultural beliefs including secular and faith-based practices.

■ In this story Patricia teaches Stewart and Winston how to make pysanky eggs from her Ukranian heritage. Invite your students to share a craft or art project from their cultural heritage.

■ Patricia went to church with her friends. Ask your students if they have ever visited different houses of worship or participated in celebrations or traditions from other cultures or religions. What did they enjoy, learn and/or find interesting?

■ Rachel 'reached out' to Mari. Explore ways to reach out and welcome those who are new to the class, school, and community. What more could the class have done to welcome Mari? Possible answers might be learn words and phrases in Greek so they could communicate with her, help her learn English words and phrases and choose someone to be a buddy. How have you reached out to someone who was new and begun to develop a relationship? How did you communicate? How could Mari have 'reached in' to her new school community? How have you 'reached in' when you were in a new situation?

Chapter 9: 'Embedding local and global issues'

Learners will:
Understand the interconnectedness and interdependence of our world.
Begin to develop an understanding of the plight of immigrants and refugees.
Begin to develop personal and social responsibility for helping immigrants and refugees.

■ Mari's family left Greece due to economic hardship in their country, and wanting a better life for their children. Help your students understand the reasons immigrants and refugees move to other countries. Help them to see the impact of war and conflict, religious oppression, drought, famine and natural disasters on the people's lives, and consequently the countries who receive them. Some of your students may have moved due to civil unrest, political upheaval or natural disasters. Be aware that they may have painful memories and powerful feelings. This is a complex issue, and children can begin to understand our responsibility to help immigrants and refugees.

9

Embedding local and global issues

Introduction

We are all increasingly aware of the range of local and global issues we are facing that threaten the sustainability of our planet. In addition to existing issues such as climate change, human rights, and war and conflict, we see water and food security emerging as critical issues to address now and for the future. Our world is faced with a growing number of environmental concerns that require awareness and urgent solutions, such as the presence of plastics in our food and water sources. Education must play a central role in developing a commitment to live, think and act in ways that lead to a sustainable future.

It is helpful to understand the role that public policy plays in our efforts. The UN was established in 1945 following the devastation of the Second World War to maintain international peace and security. UNESCO was formed soon after to promote education as a means to secure peaceful and sustainable societies. UNESCO has promoted Education for Sustainable Development (ESD) since 1992. It established the Decade of Sustainable Development (2004–2014) and it now guides the 17 Sustainable Development Goals (SDGs) for 2030 that were established in 2015. Education has been seen as central to achieving the SDGs. UNESCO advocates ESD along with Global Citizenship Education (GCE) as is stated in SDG 4, Target 4.7 (see Chapter 1).

In its 2017 publication, *Education for Sustainable Development Goals: Learning Outcomes*, UNESCO encourages ESD to be included in teacher education programmes and asks teachers to integrate ESD into the curricula. Education is seen as critical to achieve the SDGs, SDG 4 in its own right, and the other 16 SDGs as well.

As Dr Qian Tang, Assistant Director-General for Education for UNESCO states, 'Global issues such as climate change urgently require a shift in our lifestyles, and a transformation of the way we think and act. To achieve this change we need new skills, values, and attitudes that lead to more sustainable societies.'

When we educate children about global issues there is a greater focus on learning over teaching, and action is integral to the process. 'ESD is about empowering and motivating learners to become active sustainability citizens who are capable of critical thinking and able to participate in shaping a sustainable future. Pedagogical approaches that are adequate to this aim are learner-centered, action-oriented and transformative' (UNESCO, 2017).

Irina Bokova, former Director-General of UNESCO says that, 'if done right education has the power like none else to nurture empowered, reflective, engaged, and skilled citizens who can chart the way towards a safer, greener, and fairer planet for all'. (UNESCO, 2016).

We all share responsibility for addressing local and global issues

The issues that we face can only be addressed when we all take responsible action both personally and collectively. We can empower children to take responsibility locally and globally, and help them see that they can make a positive difference.

Enquiry is fundamental to addressing local and global issues

Developing interest and curiosity in local and global issues is the first step towards addressing them. We can help children see how posing relevant questions can lead to seeking viable solutions. Asking 'How can I help?' leads to sharing responsibility and taking action.

We must take action for the health and well-being of society and our planet

There is clear evidence that human activity has had a negative impact on the environment. Human actions can reverse current trends, and help heal our planet and ensure the health and well-being of present and future generations. We can help our students see that both children and adults can show leadership, and have an important role to play. We can set children on a path towards creating a better world by helping them see they do not have to wait, for example, until they become adults to have an impact.

Learning outcomes

Learners will:

- Understand the interconnectedness and interdependence of our world.
- Begin to identify and develop an understanding of contemporary global issues.
- Begin to take positive action to address global issues for a more peaceful, equitable and sustainable world.
- Begin to develop personal and social responsibility for addressing global issues.

References

Melbourne Declaration on Educational Goals for Young Australians: www.curriculum.edu.au/verve/_resources/National_Declaration_on_the_Educational_Goals_for_Young_Australians.pdf (accessed June 2017).

Rader, D and Sittig, L (2003) *New Kid in School: Using Literature to Help Children in Transition*. New York, NY: Teachers College Press.

UNESCO (2016) Education for People and Planet: Creating Sustainable Futures for All. Global Education Monitoring Report Summary. Paris: UNESCO. http://unesdoc.unesco.org/images/0024/002457/245752e.pdf (accessed January 2018).

UNESCO (2017) Education for Sustainable Development Goals: Learning Outcomes. Paris: UNESCO.

Lesson plan: Reception–Year 6

For Every Child
The Rights of the Child in Words and Pictures

by Caroline Castle
(adapted from UNICEF text)

Synopsis

This book explains the UN Convention on the Rights of the Child (UNCRC) in words and pictures. It is beautifully written in the voice of children who are speaking to adults, and illustrators from around the world have illustrated each of the 15 Articles included. The UNCRC is something I believe that all children should learn about and all schools should make visible. This book was published in 2000 and contains a moving foreword by Archbishop Desmond M Tutu with hope for the new millennium. More than ever his words of working towards peace and prosperity are needed today. This book can help children learn about the rights of the child, and encourage them to uphold the UNCRC for themselves and other children.

Learning outcomes

Learners will:

- Understand the interconnectedness and interdependence of our world.
- Begin to identify and develop an understanding of the rights of children.
- Begin to take positive action to address human rights for a more peaceful, equitable and sustainable world.
- Begin to develop personal and social responsibility for ensuring the rights of children.

Pre-reading activities

- You may wish to first read *Whoever You Are* by Mem Fox and discuss the ways that children with their differences, wherever they are from, are also the same in many ways, and precious.
- Lead a discussion about wants and needs, what they are and the difference between them. After sharing several examples, have the children work in pairs to search for images of wants and needs online and create a two-part PicCollage. You can create a class collage with younger children. Alternatively, you can use pictures that represent wants and needs, and discuss and categorise them as a class activity.
- Continue with a discussion about rights and responsibilities, what they are and how they are linked. Ask, What is a right? UNICEF explains that 'rights are things every child should have or be able to do in order to survive and grow and reach their full potential'. Share several examples of children's rights such as clean water, nutritious food, education, and a family or adults to take care of you. Point out that some needs are also rights.

  Ask, What do you think are some of the rights you have here at school?, and chart these (to learn, to be safe, to play, to be happy, and to be taken care of if you are sick).

Lesson plan: Reception–Year 6

Peace Begins with You

By Katherine Scholes
Illustrated by Robert Ingpen

Synopsis

This book provides an excellent way to approach the topic of peace with children. It clearly and simply explains the concept of peace, why conflicts occur, how they can be resolved and how to protect peace. It addresses the questions, 'What is peace?', 'Where does it come from?', 'How can you find it?' and 'How can you keep it?'. It provides suggestions for how to become a peacemaker and children are encouraged to become peacemakers as they are told that 'peace begins with you'.

Learning outcomes

Learners will:

- Understand that conflict in one country can affect the people in many others.
- Begin to develop an understanding of peace and conflict as a local and global issue.
- Begin to develop personal and social responsibility for addressing local and global issues.
- Explore ways to be a peacemaker and protect peace in your class, school, home, community and in our world.

Pre-reading activities

- Introduce the concept of peace through sharing images of peace and/or reading *A Little Peace* by Barbara Kerley or *Somewhere Today: A Book of Peace* by Shelley Moore Thomas. Discuss how we can experience both inner peace and peace around us, and how peace can mean different things to different people, and in different cultures and religions.
- Begin a chart for each of the following questions from the book:

    What is peace? (sense of calm, being loved, walking in the woods, cuddling my cat, etc.)

    Where does peace come from? (inside of us, our beliefs, our choices, our experiences, etc.)

    How can you find peace? (yoga, walking in the woods, deep breathing, working together, etc.)

    How can you keep peace? (resolving conflicts, sharing, caring about others, helping, etc.)

- Create another chart and list factors that disrupt peace in our classroom, school, home and community such as arguing, fighting, bullying, violence and meanness. For older children, chart the global issues that disrupt peace such as wars between nations, natural disasters, racial conflict and civil war.

Post-reading activities

- Add to the charts you began and include the ideas presented in the book. Make sure to include 'peace is being allowed to be different and allowing others to be different from you'.

Create two additional charts:

How can you create peace? (show kindness and respect to others, seek fair solutions, etc.)

How can you experience peace wherever you are? (breathing, managing your emotions, etc.)

Post these charts and leave them up over a period of time so the children can add new ideas.

- Discuss ways you can be peacemakers in your class and school. Have your students create posters or a class book suggesting ways to help create a more peaceful classroom and school. There are always choices; some choices threaten peace and some choices protect it. What are some choices we make to have peace at school? (to play fairly, to be kind to others, to share materials, etc.).

- Have your students create a Peace Journal and record ways they spread peace at school, at home and in the community over a week or period of time.

Suggested follow-up activities

- Read *What Does It Mean to Be Present?* by Rana DiOrio, and discuss ways to be fully present and peaceful wherever we are, even in a busy setting. Provide opportunities for your students to experience peace and share effective strategies.

- Some schools have planted a peace pole or created a peace garden, and some teachers have established a peace table or corner in their classrooms. You may wish to collaborate with your students to create a space where children can go to simply reflect, relax, and do some deep breathing to regain a sense of peace.

- Introduce your students to mindfulness exercises, and attention to their breath. If you already integrate this practice in your classroom consider having your students teach other children in other classes. They might create a video or plan an assembly to inform others of the benefits.

- Have your students research organisations that promote peace. This could include the work of the United Nations, UNICEF and others. The nonprofit Kids for Peace promotes peace through youth leadership, kindness and community service. Every January schools from around the world participate in a Great Kindness Challenge (www.kidsforpeaceglobal.org). Choose an initiative to support as a class or school.

Links with learning outcomes in other chapters

This book links with learning outcomes in the following chapters:

Chapter 6: 'Cultivating transformative beliefs, values and attitudes'

Learners will:
Begin to stand up to injustice, and speak out and take action.

- The author tells us that lasting peace can only occur when people are treated fairly. Explain that whenever we stand up for social justice, we help make the world a more peaceful place. Discuss ways the children can speak out and take action when others are being unkind or unfair, and how they can help other children find their voice.

- Discuss the difference between fair and equal, and help the children understand that being fair is making sure people have what they need, which may not be equal, and that people's needs can change.

10

Designing learning and living spaces with intercultural understanding in mind

A new year, a new beginning

I have always loved the start of a new school year and the immense joy, challenge and excitement of creating a dynamic and vibrant learning community with a new group of eager learners. It is filled with the promise and possibility of what we can learn from each other and with each other, for children and adults alike. This includes celebrating our diversity, and valuing the languages, cultures and backgrounds we all bring.

In *Valuing Languages and Cultures: The First Step Towards Developing Intercultural Understanding* (Rader, 2015) I suggested ways you can build a school community that is inclusive of the languages and cultures of your students, create culturally responsive and reflective classrooms, and teach and learn for intercultural understanding. We can demonstrate our value of languages and cultures, and develop intercultural understanding best if it is:

- embedded in all we do
- addressed explicitly, directly and indirectly
- promoted with greater mindfulness and intentionality.

As you and your colleagues look for meaningful ways to embed teaching and learning for intercultural understanding in the life of your classroom and school you will find opportunities at every turn. In this chapter I suggest ideas for setting the tone and building community, the use of physical spaces, and routines, rituals and practices that can help develop intercultural understanding. Many of these ideas appear in Tips for Teachers in *New Kid in School*, and are also embedded in the lesson plans in this book. And I know you will have many creative and innovative ideas of your own!

Setting the tone

The way we set the tone during the first days and weeks of the school year has a significant impact on the quality of the learning that takes place, and the relationships that develop between you and your students, their parents and caregivers, and between the children themselves. From the first day of school it is important that we explicitly let our students and their families know that we are interested in knowing who they are, that we value who they are and that we care about each one of them. We need to make clear our belief that everyone is important, has a place in our community and that there is something we can learn from everyone. We aim to create an environment where children and families develop the desire to know each other, value each other and care about each other, too.

Here are suggestions for you and your colleagues to consider:

■ Be explicit.

As you set out a vision for the year ahead be explicit and intentional about the values you and your school hold with regard to diversity and intercultural understanding. Explain to your students that learning about and understanding our own cultures, other cultures, and developing understanding and respect between cultures is an important part of living together in our diverse world. You might tell them that we all have something to teach each other and this year we will learn from each other about our different cultures, languages, beliefs, backgrounds and experiences. We will share our knowledge, interests and passions, as we grow and learn together. When we set a tone that is inclusive, safe, affirming and respectful, all children feel seen and are engaged with learning, each other and the life of the classroom.

■ Include families early.

Collaborate with your colleagues and administration to include parents and caregivers in the process of teaching and learning for intercultural understanding. You might plan an initial coffee morning or parent evening, apart from a back to school night, to explain the intention of your work in this area and its importance as a disposition and competence for our world. Express your hope that families will contribute to the children's learning by sharing their cultures and languages in meaningful ways, not only during school-wide or special celebrations, but also in the day-to-day life of the classroom.

■ Establish an ethos for intercultural understanding.

Teachers often begin the year by creating Essential Agreements together with their class that guide the way they and the children will learn, work and play together throughout the school year. Guide the children to establish an atmosphere of inclusion with the expectation that they will treat each other with kindness and respect from the very first day of school. Include respect for cultures and languages, diversity and difference. You may find it helpful to use the lesson plan for *The Golden Rule* as part of this process (see Chapter 6). Teachers also establish agreements for digital communications such as blogging and social media, as part of developing digital citizenship.

Using children's literature is an excellent vehicle for powerful learning. One of my favourite children's books is *Because of You* by B G Hennessy, and it lends itself well to establishing an ethos for teaching and learning for intercultural understanding. The author tells us, 'When a child is born there is one more person to love and care for, and one more person who can love and care for others.' As children grow and learn, they can also teach, share with and help others. This book is beautifully crafted, and highlights ways each one of us can contribute to our community and make a positive difference in our world.

As Junior School Principal at the International School of Florence I used this book to set the vision for the new school year with both parents and children. I read this book to parents at our first coffee morning and to children at our first whole-school assembly on the first day of school each school year. I expressed my belief that the message held true for families as well; that they, too, could make a positive difference in our school community. I told the parents their children would hear this book later that day, and I asked them to discuss its message together that night. Many parents told me of the meaningful conversations they had with their children as a result. It was a lovely way to start the school year, and one that set the tone to establish a strong learning community and ethos of collaboration.

This book may now be difficult to find; however, I urge you to try to locate a copy. Alternatively, you can search online for the video *Because of You* by B G Hennessy.

I have used it successfully in workshops and presentations with educators, and teachers have had it translated into Arabic and Dutch to use in their schools. I also suggest *BIG* by Coleen Paratore as another excellent choice. She tells us that being BIG is about being our biggest and best selves, and the BIG ways we can make a positive difference in our homes, community and world. I like the way she tells us that being BIG happens in little ways one day at a time. This is also the way we develop intercultural understanding.

Building community

There are many ways to begin to build a strong sense of community and help children get to know one another, and learn about each other's backgrounds and families. As you choose activities consider ways that the children's languages and cultures can be naturally integrated and woven into what you do. Be willing to share your own language and cultural background as well.

Here are suggestions for you and your colleagues to consider:

- Model your own respect for difference, appreciation of diversity, and interest in and curiosity about other cultures. It was established early in this book that knowing your own cultures and living your intercultural values are essential to effectively teach for intercultural understanding.

- Along with your class learn to pronounce your students' names correctly. Have students share any special meaning of their name and/or the reason it was chosen. This contributes to the children's understanding of cultural identity.

- Greet students, colleagues and parents in their home languages. Along with your students learn key words and phrases, poems and songs in the languages of the class.

- Have your students work with a partner to find out their classmate's name, place they were born, places they have lived and languages they speak. In your first class meeting have the children introduce each other and begin to note the commonalities that exist. Parents of young children often accompany their children to school for a period of orientation, and can participate in sharing together with their child.

- The first weeks of school are filled with a wide range of activities to build community and get to know one another. Some teachers have the children design a t-shirt or square for a class patchwork quilt, create identity flags or draw multicultural self-portraits, which reflect the children's personal and cultural identity.

- I often began each year with a Class Book project. The students worked in pairs to interview another child, wrote a piece about him or her, and illustrated it. This was a natural way to begin to get to know each other and foster relationships with those from different cultural backgrounds. This was a popular selection in our class library throughout the year.

- If you have many English Language Learners in your class, making About Me collages is a wonderful way for children to get to know each other and begin to see similarities and differences with their classmates. Ask the children to bring a photograph of themselves and their families. Have them collect images at home and/or school of things they like (food, activities, places, etc.) to create their collage.

- Many teachers display photographs of the children in their class. Amanda Haworth, Early Years teacher at ISS Sindelfingen, naturally embeds the value of linguistic and cultural differences. She displays photographs of her students with their names also written in their home language script, the flags from the countries they are from, and their birthdate written in the format of their home countries.

The physical space

'There are three teachers of children; adults, other children and the environment,' said Italian educator, Loris Malaguzzi, who developed the *Reggio Emilia* approach to learning, where young children are encouraged to explore their physical environment and engage in self-directed tasks. The way we design and plan our physical spaces can help nurture intercultural understanding in our students.

- Label your classroom in the children's languages. Many schools have the word *Welcome* posted in reception and on classroom doors in the different languages of the children in the class or school. Ensure that signs, notices, newsletters and other communication are also written in the languages of the school. Include multicultural and multilingual displays, resources and literature, photographs, projects, dual-language identity texts, bilingual and multilingual publishing and more, which convey the value of its diversity. Use your sense of the aesthetic and with your students consider ways to use fabric, artwork and cultural artefacts in classroom and learning spaces. Invite your students to contribute items from their cultures to help create the cultural fabric of your classroom.

- Ensure that cultural learning is accurate and authentic and does not inadvertently reinforce stereotypes. Select books and resources carefully, and evaluate them critically. Include positive images of children and adults from different countries and cultures. Include images of innovators, great thinkers, writers and artists in our world of different races and ethnicities. Include materials with accurate and positive images of gender, gender identification, LGTBQ, body size and shape, age, socioeconomic status, ability, and physical and learning differences.

- In many schools large TV screens are displayed in prominent public spaces to promote service learning and social action projects, inform the community of children's work with NGOs, and display photographs or play videos of events showcasing the diversity of the school. They could be used to communicate and celebrate the excellent intercultural learning that is happening in your school and in the languages of the school.

- For younger children consider ways your dramatic play area could reflect different cultures including those present in the classroom. Include clothing, food containers labelled in different languages, and cooking and eating utensils. This provides an authentic opportunity to discuss similarities and differences between cultural objects and practices, and experience using them.

- Create baskets or discovery boxes where children can explore different languages through printed text, including braille and sign language charts. Create learning stations where children can experiment with different kinds of writing and writing tools.

- I loved an idea I saw from a Grade 1 teacher at Berlin Metropolitan School. She allocated wall space for each child to hang a clipboard and the children could post whatever they like. There were personal photographs of friends and family, and pets on display. Model this with a clipboard for yourself.

- Provide a notice board space in your classroom where students can bring brochures or art postcards from cultural events they have attended. Initiate a whole-school notice board that celebrates your multicultural community and ask families and faculty to post the cultural events happening in your city or town.

- In your school plan seating arrangements and common areas that invite collaboration, group work, sharing of ideas and developing relationships. Many schools are designing their physical spaces with flexible learning environments in mind. The Elementary School campus at the

American School of Bombay has been designed to give teachers and students flexibility for collaboration. The library has been decentralised and each floor has its own designated pod called the iCommons. Each pod has its own library and maker spaces. Grades 1–5 are 1:1 with laptops and children in Grades 4 and 5 bring their own laptops from home. Large screen TVs are utilised throughout the school.

■ Some schools have created Outdoor Learning Environments and garden spaces that also promote environmental education and sustainable living practices. Children develop an appreciation and respect for the natural world and are inspired to take steps to protect the local and global environment.

Visual images are powerful and convey our values and beliefs in meaningful ways.

What we want to see is the richness and vibrancy of our schools in evidence for all to appreciate and enjoy.

Routines, rituals and practices

■ I have always found it very helpful to ask the parents and/or children to complete a Personal Interest Inventory at the beginning of the school year. This can be completed in English or in the child's home language. It has been an invaluable source of information, and I have referred to it time and time again throughout the year when I was looking for a book to engage a reluctant reader, and ways to personalise learning.

■ Many schools have families complete a Home Language Survey to provide information about the languages spoken at home, and your students' language skills and needs. This would be very useful in any school and will help inform your planning.

■ The transition to a new school can be particularly daunting for children who do not speak the language of instruction and/or host country language. Schools that reflect and celebrate the languages and cultures of their students make them feel welcome, affirm their identity and ease the transition process. Engage your students in developing ways to welcome, support and include children who arrive and do not speak the same language. This may include assigning a buddy, creating a dual language phrasebook or welcome guide to your class, school and/or local community in multiple languages. This develops empathy, respect and responsibility, which lead to intercultural understanding.

■ Look for and provide learning opportunities that recognise and honour the cultural traditions of the children in your class, school community and the wider world in everyday situations, not only during celebrations or designated UN Days.

■ Share your knowledge of other languages and cultures. Read to children in the languages you speak, and invite students and parents to do so as well. Invite students and parents to bring literature resources to share in their home languages that relate to topics being studied, and teach each other key vocabulary in their own languages. Children will find it interesting to learn words in new languages and this helps them see that learning takes place in all languages.

■ Recognise translanguaging as a natural practice for language learners and include it in your classroom (see Chapter 4).

■ Make use of the opportunities for authentic cultural learning that exist within your school community. Invite parents, teaching and non-teaching staff to help you and your students learn about their cultures, including their languages and beliefs. Include the different ways birthdays, weddings and other rites of passage are celebrated, as well as dance, art, music, drama, games and storytelling traditions.

- Learn about your students' home cultures and languages, and include them in authentic ways in the learning engagements you plan, the resources you select, and the examples you use and references you make in your instruction. When we honour and recognise our students' cultures, languages and identities we connect with them more deeply, which leads to an increase in student learning, achievement and well-being.

- Consider keeping a class Awareness Log where you and the children record acts of kindness and thoughtfulness you have observed during the school day. These are shared at the end of the day.

- Collaborate with your colleagues to establish cross-grade buddies, which has enormous benefits for children of all ages. Intercultural and cross-age friendships develop, and the children take pride in learning from and teaching each other.

- Incorporate local and global issues in your curriculum – where possible in the core curriculum, or address them in circle time, morning meeting discussions and activities or school-wide initiatives. Use circle time or morning meetings to talk about and explore the components of intercultural understanding and relevant current events.

- Help establish and grow a multilingual library in your classroom where children have easy access to books in different languages. Ask parents for donations of children's books, magazines and newspapers in their home languages. Include multiple copies of well-known, favourite children's books in multiple languages such as *The Dot* or *The Giving Tree*.

- Consider these learning engagements some of which are integrated into the lesson plans in this book:

    Literature discussions and projects that help develop multiple perspectives, critical thinking, intercultural sensitivity, and historical, cultural or personal perspectives.

    Writing workshop: include poetry, memoir, narrative, etc.

    Family history projects.

    Personal and Cultural Identity Maps.

    Collage journals.

    Multicultural self-portraits.

    Personal time lines.

    Study of countries and cultures, and belief systems.

Closing

We all have a shared responsibility to create caring and compassionate school communities where all children and adults feel affirmed, valued and thrive. You are encouraged to draw on your own experiences and creativity to create innovative and meaningful ways to include the languages and cultures of your school community. The possibilities are endless and the rewards are great. When we work together to value each other with mindfulness and intentionality we all benefit immensely.

(Rader, 2015)

PAUSE FOR REFLECTION

How are children's cultures and languages reflected in the life of your classroom and school?

How can and do you demonstrate your value of cultural and linguistic differences in your practice?

How can the classroom and school spaces reflect the languages and cultures of the school community?

How can we make difference visible and cherished in our classrooms and school spaces?

References

Hennessy, B G (2009) *Because of You*. Cambridge, MA: Candlewick Press.

Paratore, C (2013) *BIG*. Belvedere, CA: Little Pickle Press.

Rader, D and Sittig, L (2003) *New Kid in School: Using Literature to Help Children in Transition*. New York, NY: Teachers College Press.

Rader, D (2015) Valuing Languages and Cultures: The First Step Towards Developing Intercultural Understanding. *International Schools Journal*, Vol. XXXIV, No. 2 (April) p. 17–22.

11

Applying our knowledge, using our skills and living our values

Introduction

We know that developing knowledge and understanding, beliefs, values and attitudes, and intercultural, interpersonal and life skills for intercultural understanding is a lifelong process for everyone. When we recognise the importance of developing this disposition and competence it becomes a natural part of the way we live our lives, and by extension we model intercultural understanding for others. We seek opportunities to collaborate with colleagues, families and children in our schools to help embed intercultural understanding in the life of our classrooms and school community. We support learning opportunities that emerge from the children as part of our work together. And we share our personal and professional networks to create connections with educators and students, and deepen learning for everyone.

Educational researcher, John Hattie (2015), has identified the importance of collaborative expertise to maximise teachers' impact on student learning. When educators collaborate, share expertise and have a shared understanding of learning outcomes everyone benefits. I believe this holds true for teaching and learning for intercultural understanding as well. All that is needed is our belief in the value of intercultural understanding, commitment to nurture its development, and our creativity and initiative.

The following are excellent examples of collaboration between colleagues that support intercultural understanding and which grew out of their shared commitment and spirit of collegiality.

The Story Behind My Name Project

Jeffrey Brewster, former Elementary School Librarian, and Miles Madison, former Grade 2 teacher, at the International School of Brussels, worked together to develop *The Story Behind My Name Project* as part of building community at the beginning of the school year. Both Jeffrey and Miles are deeply committed to children's well-being, and social and emotional learning. They share the value of developing character in children, believe that identity is important and recognise that our names are personal and meaningful. They also share a love of children's literature.

They chose several literature selections related to children's names, which were first introduced in the library session. Good literature lends itself to multiple readings and these books were then revisited in the classroom. Jeffrey and Miles created a range of literacy and maths activities, and as a culminating project collaborated with the children's families to create a Class Book that contained the story behind each child's name.

Helping to create a better world

Introduction

Inspired educators around the world are integrating ways to develop intercultural understanding into their curricula, large and small, and in schools large and small. In this chapter I have included examples of best practices and initiatives from a range of schools from different countries and on different continents that illustrate meaningful ways to promote teaching and learning for intercultural understanding. Whether they are an international, or national state or public school they offer examples that can be integrated into any school anywhere. I am grateful for their contributions to this chapter and hope they inspire you as they have inspired me.

When we make teaching and learning for intercultural understanding a priority we find ways to include and embed it in all that we do in the life of the school. The schools highlighted here do just that. You are encouraged to build on what you already have in place, and consider similar practices and initiatives for your own context and community.

The American International School of Lusaka, Zambia

The American International School of Lusaka (AISL), located on the outskirts of Lusaka, embeds an appreciation and respect for Zambian culture in all aspects of the school. Primary Assistant Principal and PYP Coordinator, Chye de Ryckel, tells about the programmes that support intercultural understanding.

The school environment is rich with Zambian colours and patterns, from the beautiful *chitenge* cloth to the natural materials used in the classrooms. The students sing the school song, which is a call and response song including lyrics in both English and Nyanja, one of the local languages commonly spoken around Lusaka.

Educators ensure that the Units of Inquiry in their IBPYP Programme of Inquiry provide rich opportunities to develop knowledge, understanding and appreciation of the host country, Zambia. Teachers, teaching assistants, parents and community members collaborate with the children and each other to plan enriching learning experiences. They utilise the local environment and its resources, and meaningful and memorable learning experiences have included:

- planning a journey to visit one child's home in the African bush where giraffes, zebras, bush-buck, and warthogs roam freely in his garden and the surrounding environment (Kindergarten 'Where we are in place and time' unit where students learned about how we learn about the world through the journeys we take)

- going on 'safari' to a friend's house to observe the bio garden (Preschool 'Sharing the planet' unit where students learned about the world through scientific investigation)

- going inside a village mud hut and learning how it's built (Grade 1 'Where we are in place and time' unit where students studied homes around the world, starting with our own homes and homes in the immediate environment)

- observing animals at the National Park (Grade 5 'Sharing the planet' unit about biodiversity)

- touring the High Court of Zambia when learning about city systems (Grade 3 'How we organise ourselves' unit about interdependent systems)

- visiting the Kariba Dam and learning about hydroelectricity (Grade 4 'How the world works' unit about energy).

Students regularly take action in the local community, acting on areas where they see great need.

RHO Appleseed Community Center: Inspired to make a difference in the lives of vulnerable children in our local community, an AISL teaching couple started the RHO Appleseed School, which later became the Appleseed Community Center. AISL students regularly volunteer at RHO Appleseed playing chess, reading together, and engaging in other social activities such as dance lessons. This has been a highlight for children at RHO Appleseed as they develop their English language skills, and spend time with kind and caring people. Teachers say this fills the hearts of their students and encourages the development of empathy, respect and compassion.

Adopt an Elephant: Partnering with the local organisation, Game Rangers International (GRI), Grade 2 students have learned valuable lessons about how to live peacefully with the largest land-dwelling animals on our planet. They learn how there is a struggle in the sharing of natural resources, and that some people choose to poach because they see no other option. They begin to understand and consider the different sides to poaching and are moved to take action when they learn a common result of poaching is orphaned elephants. GRI rescues these orphans and works for months and years to successfully reintroduce them to Kafue National Park. Grade 2 students learn about this issue and raise awareness about it in the community.

Through these projects students are able to see how they can make a positive difference in the local community and help teach others about important issues.

American School of Bombay (ASB), Mumbai, India

The American School of Bombay (ASB) is a highly multicultural and multilingual international school located in Mumbai. It is fully committed to providing opportunities for its students to engage with the host country and culture, and enhance the lives of others. Each grade in the Elementary School is connected with a local Non-Governmental Organization (NGO) in Mumbai. These are examples of its impactful learning in Grades 4 and 5.

Grade 5 is connected with the ACORN Foundation (India) and the Dharavi Project. The Acorn Foundation provides after-school activities for children who live in Dharavi, one of the world's largest slums, and a major hub for the recycling industry.

The children learn about the history and work of the foundation, and visit Dharavi to see the waste management business and recycling that takes place. Children from Dharavi visit ASB and the children play 'getting to know you' games, sing songs and do craft projects together. This gives the ASB students an opportunity to use some of the Hindi they are learning through the school's Host Country Studies and Hindi Program.

During the 2016–2017 school year the children in Dharavi created a music group, Dharavi Rocks, using recycled rubbish bins, oil cans and bottles to make music. Grade 5 students decided to use the money they raised from their Business Fair to buy additional instruments for Dharavi Rocks. At the end of the year the children had a musical celebration together and the children performed for each other.

is awarded to classes where the most children come to school by 'active travel' such as scooter, bicycle or on foot.

The children from Years 3–6 participate in the innovative Stephanie Alexander Garden Project Foundation Kitchen Garden Programme. Here they learn about the natural world and its resources, how to care for the garden and compost, and experience first-hand the pleasure of growing, preparing and sharing food together. They plan menus based on the seasonal availability of the crops they grow and prepare dishes from other cultures to present cultural differences as fascinating, rather than strange.

Celebrating diversity

National Reconciliation Week is celebrated across Australia between 27th May and 3rd June each year to mark the Referendum of 1967 to formally recognise their indigenous peoples and the Mabo High Court decision to recognise the land rights of the Meriam people, traditional owners of the Murray Islands. Its purpose is to acknowledge wrongs that have been done in the past and move forward in ways that build respect and trust between the wider Australian community and Aboriginal and Torres Strait Islander peoples. While it remains controversial it was a step in the right direction and activism for the equal rights of indigenous people continues today. Many programmes exist to contribute to reconciliation and break down stereotypes and discrimination, and develop knowledge and pride in the histories, identities, cultures and contributions of the First Australians.

The school invites an Aboriginal elder to talk to the children about Aboriginal culture, share dream stories, and perform a Smoking Ceremony where the children and adults walk through the smoke as a spiritual cleansing.

The school celebrates Harmony Day on 21st March to coincide with the UN International Day for the Elimination of Racial Discrimination. It honours Australia's cultural diversity, and promotes inclusiveness, respect and a sense of belonging for everyone.

Countries and cultures are celebrated during Multicultural Week, and are integrated into the learning areas. Diversity in family structures is discussed every year, and children understand that there are many different kinds of families.

Closing

Developing the disposition and competence for intercultural understanding is one of the most important ways we can educate children for a better world. I suggest you create a checklist of practices and programmes for your particular school and context. You are encouraged to work with your colleagues to reflect on what you are already doing in your own school, and consider ways your school can enhance teaching and learning for intercultural understanding.

Reference

Gallagher, E (2008) *Equal Rights to the Curriculum: Many Languages One Message.* Clevedon: Multilingual Matters.

Appendix A

Children's literature for developing intercultural understanding

There is a wealth of excellent children's literature that supports teaching and learning for intercultural understanding, and addresses the components of the *Framework for Developing Intercultural Understanding* (Rader, 2016). These are titles I think are particularly useful, and can be easily integrated into the curriculum. Picture books have far reaching appeal and can be used effectively across grade/year levels. The titles marked with an asterisk (*) are those featured in the lesson plans in this book.

Picture books

Ajmera, M and Ivanko, J D (1999) *To Be a Kid*. Watertown, MA: Charlesbridge.
*Aliki (1998) *Marianthe's Story: Painted Words and Spoken Memories*. New York: Greenwillow Books.
*Bang, M (2015) *When Sophie's Feelings Are Really, Really Hurt*. New York, NY: The Blue Sky Press.
Buller, L (2005) *A Faith Like Mine*. New York, NY: DK Publishing.
*Bunting, E (2006) *One Green Apple*. New York, NY: Clarion Books.
*Castle, C (2002) *For Every Child: The Rights of the Child in Words and Pictures*. London: Red Fox Books and UNICEF.
*Cooper, I (2007) *The Golden Rule*. New York, NY: Abrams Books for Young Readers.
*Choi, Y (2001) *The Name Jar*. New York, NY: Dragonfly Books.
De Zutter, H (1993) *Who Says a Dog Goes Bow-Wow?* New York, NY: Delacorte Press.
DiOrio, R (2016) *What Does It Mean to Be An Entrepreneur?* San Francisco, CA: Little Pickle Press.
*DiOrio, R (2009) *What Does It Mean to Be Global?* Belvedere, CA: Little Pickle Press.
DiOrio, R (2010) *What Does It Mean to Be Green?* Belvedere, CA: Little Pickle Press.
DiOrio, R (2015) *What Does It Mean to Be Kind?* San Francisco, CA: Little Pickle Press.
DiOrio, R (2010) *What Does It Mean to Be Present?* San Francisco, CA: Little Pickle Press.
DiOrio, R (2011) *What Does It Mean to Be Safe?* Belvedere, CA: Little Pickle Press.
Dooley, N (1991) *Everybody Eats Rice*. Minneapolis, MN: Carolrhoda Books.
Dooley, N (1996) *Everybody Bakes Bread*. Minneapolis, MN: Carolrhoda Books.
Dooley, N (2000) *Everybody Serves Soup*. Minneapolis, MN: Carolrhoda Books.
*Fanelli, S (1995) *My Map Book*. New York, NY: HarperCollins.
Fleischman, P (1997) *Seedfolks*. New York, NY: HarperCollins.
Foreman, M (2015) *The Seeds of Friendship*. London: Walker Books, Ltd.
Fox, M (1997) *Whoever You Are*. New York, NY: Harcourt Books.
Hamanaka, S (1994) *All the Colors of the Earth*. New York, NY: William Morrow and Company, Inc.
Hennessy, B G (2005) *Because of You*. Cambridge, MA: Candlewick Press.
*Hoffman, M (1991) *Amazing Grace*. New York, NY: Dial Books for Young Readers.
Hoffman, M (2002) *The Color of Home*. New York, NY: Dial Books for Young Readers.
Kerley, B (2007) *A Little Peace*. Washington, DC: National Geographic Society.
Kerley, B (2002) *A Cool Drink of Water*. Washington, DC: National Geographic Society.
Kerley, B (2005) *You and Me TOGETHER: Moms, Dads and Kids Around the World*. Washington, DC: National Geographic Society.

Kerley, B (2009) *One World, One Day*. Washington, DC: National Geographic Society.

Kissinger, K (2014) *All the Colors We Are: The Story of How We Get Our Skin Color/Todos los colores de nuestra piel: La storia depor qué tenemos dierentes colores de piel*. St Paul, MN: Redleaf Press.

Kobald, I and Blackwood, F (2014) *My Two Blankets*. New York, NY: Houghton Mifflin Harcourt.

Kroll, V L (1997) *Hands!* Honesdale, PA: Boyds Mill Press.

Lionni, L (1959) *Little Blue and Little Yellow*. New York, NY: HarperCollins Children's Books.

Milway, K S (2008) *One Hen: How One Small Loan Made a Big Difference*. Toronto, ON: Kids Can Press.

Morris, A (1989) *Bread, Bread, Bread*. New York, NY: HarperTrophy Books.

Morris, A (1989) *Hats, Hats, Hats*. New York, NY: Mulberry Books.

Morris, A (1992) *Houses and Homes*. New York, NY: HarperTrophy Books.

Morris, A (1995) *Shoes, Shoes, Shoes*. New York, NY: Mulberry Books.

Morris, A (1990) *On the Go*. New York, NY: Mulberry Books.

Otoshi, K (2008) *One*. San Rafael, CA: KO Kids Books.

Paratore, C (2012) *BIG*. Belvedere, CA: Little Pickle Press.

Parr, T (2001) *It's Okay to be Different*. New York, NY: Little Brown Books for Young Readers.

Parr, T (2003) *The Family Book*. New York, NY: Little Brown and Company.

Parr, T (2004) *The Peace Book*. New York, NY: Little Brown Books for Young Readers.

★Polacco, P (1992) *Chicken Sunday*. New York, NY: Putnam & Grosset.

Polacco, P (1992) *Mrs Katz and Tush*. New York, NY: Bantam Doubleday Dell Books for Young Readers.

★Reynolds, B (1998) *Tokyo Friends: Tokyo no Tomodachi*. Boston, MA: Tuttle Publishing.

Rosen, M (1992) *Elijah's Angel*. New York, NY: Voyager Books.

Say, A (1993) *Grandfather's Journey*. New York, NY: Houghton Mifflin.

★Scholes, K (1989) *Peace Begins with You*. San Francisco, CA: Sierra Club Books.

Silver, G (2009) *Anh's Anger*. Berkeley, CA: Plum Blossom Books.

Smith, C R Jr (2013) *I am the World*. New York, NY: Atheneum Books for Young Readers.

★Strauss, R (2007) *One Well: The Story of Water on Earth*. Toronto, ON: Kids Can Press.

Thomas, S M (1998) *Somewhere Today: A Book of Peace*. Morton Grove, IL: Albert Whitman & Company.

★Thong, R (2008) *Wish: Wishing Traditions Around the World*. San Francisco, CA: Chronicle Books LLC.

Tyler, M (2005) *The Skin You Live In*. Chicago, IL: Chicago Children's Museum.

UNICEF (Amanda Raynor, Editor) (2006) *A Life Like Mine: How Children Live Around the World*. New York, NY: DK.

Winter, J (2008) *Wangiri's Trees of Peace: A True Story from Africa*. Orlando, FL: Harcourt, Inc.

Woodruff, E (2006) *Small Beauties: The Journey of Darcy Heart O'Hara*. New York, NY: Alfred A Knopf.

★Woodson, J (2012) *Each Kindness*. New York, NY: Nancy Paulsen Books.

★Woodson, J (2001) *The Other Side*. New York, NY: GP Putnam's Sons.

Zalben, J B (2006) *Paths to Peace: People Who Changed the World*. New York, NY: Dutton Children's Books.

Upper primary

★Ada, F A and Zubizarreta, G M (2013) *Dancing Home*. New York, NY: First Atheneum Books for Young Readers.

Ada, F A (1995) *My Name is María Isabel*. New York, NY: First Atheneum Books for Young Readers.

Lai, T (2011) *Inside Out and Back Again*. New York, NY: HarperCollins Children's Books.

Lord, B B (1984) *In the Year of the Boar and Jackie Robinson*. New York, NY: HarperCollins.

Park, L S (2015) *A Long Walk to Water*. New York, NY: Houghton Mifflin Harcourt.

Woodson, J (2016) *Brown Girl Dreaming*. New York, NY: Puffin Books.

Appendix B
Multimedia resources

These are videos, films and music that help promote intercultural understanding. All websites were accessed in January 2018.

https://artsedge.kennedy-center.org/educators

Arts Edge is the Kennedy Center's free digital resource for teaching and learning in, through and about the arts. This website provides excellent ideas and resources for honouring your students' unique cultural heritage, and creating authentic and memorable cultural experiences for children through the arts. Arts integration is promoted through music, dance, the visual arts, theatre and literature.

www.duolingo.com

The DuoLingo website provides lessons to learn 23 different languages where children in K-12 and adults can practise language learning.

www.commonlit.org

CommonLit is a free collection of fiction and non-fiction for 5th–12th grade classrooms. There is a range of useful texts for Upper Primary that supports teaching and learning for intercultural understanding.

http://mediasmarts.ca

MediaSmarts is Canada's Centre for digital and media literacy. This website promotes diversity and inclusion online, and provides resources for K-12 educators and parents that address issues in digital and media literacy such as stereotypes, gender representation and cyberbullying. MediaSmarts also raises public awareness of the importance of appropriate internet usage for children and youth, and engages in ongoing research.

www.nfb.ca

The National Film Board of Canada has a wide range of films that address many components of intercultural understanding.

www.poets.org

Poets.org is the largest poetry website with resources for teachers to integrate poetry into the curriculum. There are poems that address many of the themes that pertain to intercultural understanding such as identity, gratitude, social justice, hope and gender.

www.independent.co.uk/news/uk/home-news/seven-year-old-girl-anu-activity-prosthetic-blade-best-reaction-friends-birmingham-a7716046.html

This video is featured in Chapter 7, 'Engaging with difference', and can be used to discuss creating an inclusive community.

www.edutopia.org/blog/film-festival-bullying-prevention-upstanders

This is a collection of videos that can be used to stimulate conversations about how to become an upstander against bullying.

We dine together

www.youtube.com/watch?v=QdDa2outstI

This video is featured in the lesson plan, *Each Kindness,* in Chapter 6, and can be used to inspire ideas for creating an inclusive community in your school.

www.songsforteaching.com/themeunits/peacetheme.htm

These are songs for peace and you can also find songs about community.

www.soundsofhope.org

This is an international summer preforming arts camp for children aged ten and older in St Paul, MN, and provides a profound experience of intercultural learning.

Appendix C
Web-based resources

This is a list of useful websites to support teaching and learning for intercultural understanding. They provide resources for educators and students that help develop global citizenship and global competence. All websites were accessed in January 2018.

http://asiasociety.org/education/educators

The Asia Society is a global non-profit organisation focused on building understanding between the Asia Pacific region and the West. The Center for Global Education provides a wealth of resources for educators to help develop global competence, and includes lesson plans, curriculum resources, and Web 2.0 tools and sites.

http://character.org/lessons/lesson-plans

Schools share lesson plans and projects that develop character in children.

https://facinghistory.org

This website provides excellent background knowledge and materials for secondary school students and educators on racism, prejudice, and antisemitism to counter bigotry and hatred; many of which can be adapted for primary school.

http://eithnegallagher.net

Eithne Gallagher promotes interlingual teaching and learning. Read about her exemplary series of books, *The Glitterlings,* that promotes language learning, diversity and inclusion.

www.globalgiving.org

GlobalGiving is the largest global crowdfunding community connecting non-profits, donors, and companies in nearly every country. They provide tips, tools, and resources for non-profits, donors, and companies making the world a better place.

www.iearn.org

iEARN is a non-profit organisation that engages students and teachers in collaborative project work worldwide.

www.jubileecentre.ac.uk

The Jubilee Centre for Character and Virtues at the University of Birmingham provides excellent resources for teaching character education.

www.kidsforpeaceglobal.org

This organisation helps 'create peace through youth leadership, community service, global friendships and thoughtful acts of kindness.' It has established and promotes the Peace Pledge Program and the Great Kindness Challenge.

www.kindness.org

kindness.org is a digital platform designed to reach across oceans and time zones to inspire small ripples of everyday compassion. It suggests small acts of kindness.

https://mindfulnessinschools.org

Mindfulness in Schools Project (MiSP) is a UK-based charity that supports educators and children in the teaching of mindfulness practice in schools.

https://nobully.org

No Bully provides resources for students and educators in its aim to fulfill its mission to eradicate bullying and cyberbullying among youth worldwide. The activity for building compassion, *Just Like Me,* is featured in Chapter 7, 'Engaging with difference'.

www.oxfam.org.uk/education/global-citizenship/global-citizenship-guides

Oxfam Education offers a wide range of ideas, resources and support for developing global learning and global citizenship in the classroom and the whole school.

www.racismnoway.com.au

Racism. No way! promotes anti-racism education programmes, strategies and resources which are appropriate for use in Australian schools. Most of these can be adapted for use in your context.

www.rootsandshoots.org

Jane Goodall's Roots & Shoots is a youth service programme for young people of all ages. Its mission is to foster respect and compassion for all living things, to promote understanding of all cultures and beliefs, and to inspire each individual to take action to make the world a better place for people, other animals and the environment.

www.savethechildren.org.uk/what-we-do/childrens-rights/united-nations-convention-of-the-rights-of-the-child

This website provides information about the UNCRC and the ways Save the Children works to protect the rights of children around the world.

www.teachingforchange.org

Teaching for Change provides teachers and parents with the tools to create schools where students learn to read, write and change the world. You will find useful lists of multicultural and social justice books and articles to inform your practice and to use with your students.

www.tolerance.org

Teaching Tolerance provides excellent classroom resources for promoting diversity, equity and justice, and ensuring that all children are included, respected and valued.

www.understandingprejudice.org

This website provides resources for students and teachers that address prejudice and social justice.

https://en.unesco.org/gced

This website provides a wealth of excellent resources for Global Citizenship Education.

www.unicef.org

Discover the ways that UNICEF advocates for the rights of children around the globe to protect the life of every child, every day.

www.virtuesproject.com

This website provides excellent resources for practising the virtues for children and adults.

www.waterforsouthsudan.org

This website supports the work of Water for South Sudan (WFSS), a not-for-profit corporation which was started by Salva Dut, one of the 'Lost Boys of Sudan'. WFSS drills wells and provides clean water for the people in South Sudan. Teacher and student resources that support Salva's story and *A Long Walk to Water* by Linda Sue Park are provided.

www.welcomingschools.org

This website provides excellent resources for creating inclusive, safe and welcoming schools for all children and their families.

Appendix D
Resources for educators and parents

This is a list of recommended books, TED Talks, videos and articles that support teaching and learning for intercultural understanding. All websites were accessed in January 2018.

Books

Chumak-Horbatsch, R (2012) *Linguistically Appropriate Practice.* Toronto: University of Toronto Press.

Derman-Sparks, K, LeeKeenan, D and Nimmo, J (2015) *Leading Anti-Bias Early Childhood Programs: A Guide for Change.* New York, NY: Teachers College Press and Washington, DC: NAEYC.

Gallagher, E (2008) *Equal Rights to the Curriculum: Many Languages One Message.* Clevedon: Multilingual Matters.

Heitner, D (2016) *Screenwise: Helping Kids Thrive (and Survive) in their Digital World.* New York, NY: Bibliomotion, Inc.

Meyer, E (2014) *The Culture Map: Breaking Through the Invisible Boundaries of Global Business.* New York, NY: PublicAffairs.

Nhat Hanh, T (2012) *A Handful of Quiet: Happiness in Four Pebbles.* Berkeley, CA: Plum Blossom Books.

Nhat Hanh, T (2008) *Mindful Movements: Ten Exercises for Well-Being.* Berkeley, CA: Parallax Press.

Nhat Hanh, T and the Plum Village Community (2011) *Planting Seeds: Practicing Mindfulness With Children.* Berkeley, CA: Parallax Press.

Nieto, S (2013) *Finding Joy in Teaching Students of Diverse Backgrounds: Culturally Responsive and Socially Just Practices in U.S. Classrooms.* Portsmouth, NH: Heinemann.

Pollock, D and Van Reken, R (2009) *Third Culture Kids: Growing Up Among Worlds.* Boston, MA: Nicholas Brealey Publishing.

Popov, K L and Popov, D (1997) *The Family Virtues Guide: Simple Ways to Bring Out the Best in Our Children and Ourselves.* New York, NY: Plume.

Popov, K L (2000) *The Virtues Project Educator's Guide.* Austin, TX: pro.ed

Powell, O and Powell, W (2010) *Becoming an Emotionally Intelligent Teacher.* Alexandria, VA: ASCD.

Powell, O and Powell, W (2011) *How to Teach Now: Five Keys to Personalized Learning in the Global Classroom.* Thousand Oaks, CA: Corwin.

Rader, D and Sittig, L (2003) *New Kid in School: Using Literature to Help Children in Transition.* New York, NY: Teachers College Press.

Rechtschaffen, D (2014) *The Way of Mindful Education: Cultivating Well-Being in Teachers and Students.* New York, NY: WW Norton & Co, Inc.

Rechtschaffen, D (2016) *The Mindful Education Workbook: Lessons for Teaching Mindfulness to Students.* New York, NY: WW Norton & Co, Inc.

Reimers, F., Chopra, V., Chung, C. K., Higdon, J., and O'Donnell, E. B. (2016) *Empowering Global Citizens: A World Course.* SC: CreateSpace Independent Publishing Platform.

Ribble, Mike (2015) *Digital Citizenship in Schools: Nine Elements All Students Should Know.* Arlington, VA: ISTE.

Snel, E (2013) *Sitting Still Like a Frog: Mindfulness Exercises for Kids (and Their Parents).* Boston, MA: Shambala.

Tavanger, H S and Mladic-Morales, B (2014) *The Global Education Toolkit for Elementary Learners.* Thousand Oaks, CA: Corwin. (This book provides a wealth of resources and activities that add a global dimension to your existing curriculum. It includes a wide range of technology tools, resources and ideas for global collaboration.)

Tavanger, H S (2009) *Growing Up Global: Raising Children to be at Home in the World.* New York, NY: Ballantine Books. (This is an excellent resource for both parents and educators, and provides meaningful learning and life experiences to create inclusive communities and develop an intercultural perspective.)

Weil, Z (2003) *Above All Be Kind: Raising a Humane Child in Challenging Times*. Gabriola Island, BC: New Society Publishers.
Weil, Z (2016) *The World Becomes What We Teach: Educating a Generation of Solutionaries*. New York, NY: Lantern Books.
York, S (2016) *Roots and Wing: Affirming Culture and Preventing Bias in Early Childhood*. St Paul, MN: Redleaf Press.

TED Talks and videos

Adiche, Chimamanda Ngozi, TED Talk, 'The Danger of a Single Story' July 2009:
www.ted.com/talks/chimamanda_adichie_the_danger_of_a_single_story

Chumak-Horbatsch, Roma PhD, 'Linguistically Appropriate Practice (LAP)':
www.youtube.com/watch?v=wLod5d9mT98

Dass, Angelica, TED Talk, 'The Beauty of Human Skin in Every Color' February 2016:
www.ted.com/talks/angelica_dass_the_beauty_of_human_skin_in_every_color?referrer=playlist-413

Meyers, Verna, TED Talk, 'How to Overcome Our Biases? Walk Boldly Toward Them' November 2014:
www.ted.com/talks/verna_myers_how_to_overcome_our_biases_walk_boldly_toward_them

Robinson, Mary, TED Talk, 'Why Climate Change is a Threat to Human Rights':
www.ted.com/talks/mary_robinson_why_climate_change_is_a_threat_to_human_rights

Selasi, Taiye, TED Talk, 'Don't Ask Where I'm From, Ask Where I'm Local' October 2014:
www.ted.com/talks/taiye_selasi_don_t_ask_where_i_m_from_ask_where_i_m_a_local

Sivers, Derek, TED Talk, 'Weird or just different?' November 2009:
www.ted.com/talks/derek_sivers_weird_or_just_different

Stark, Kio, TED Talk, 'Why you should talk to strangers' February 2016:
www.ted.com/talks/kio_stark_why_you_should_talk_to_strangers?referrer=playlist-413

Tanaka, Ken, 'What Kind of Asian Are You?': https://www.youtube.com/watch?v=DWynJkN5HbQ

Tanaka, Ken, 'But We're Speaking Japanese!': www.youtube.com/watch?v=oLt5qSm9U80

Weil, Zoe, 'The World Becomes What You Teach': www.youtube.com/watch?v=t5HEV96dIuY

Articles

https://socialjusticebooks.org/guide-for-selecting-anti-bias-childrens-books
Louise Derman-Sparks suggests ways to select anti-bias children's books.

https://ofeliagarciadotorg.files.wordpress.com/2011/02/translanguaging-in-schools-subiendo-y-bajando-bajando-y-subi-endo-as-afterword.pdf
In this article Professor Ofelia García discusses translanguaging in schools.

Grosjean, F (2nd March 2016). 'What is Translanguaging?' interview: www.psychologytoday.com/blog/life-bilingual/201603/what-is-translanguaging

www.elleuk.com/life-and-culture/news/a26855/more-than-an-other
In this article Meghan Markle discusses her biracial identity with an insightful perspective.

Appendix E
Partnering with families

Developing intercultural understanding is most effective if we work together with children and their families. These are suggestions for ways to develop strong family partnerships, and engage parents and caregivers in developing intercultural understanding.

Parent education

Communicate to families your commitment as a school to developing intercultural understanding within the school community, and its importance as a disposition and competence for our world. As I suggested in Chapter 10, it is helpful to plan a parent education session early in the school year to explain the intention of your work in this area, and encourage family participation in sharing their languages and cultures. Invite guest speakers to address topics such as anti-bias education, bullying, language learning and intercultural awareness. Invite local community members to share their cultures, languages and stories.

AoEs

Many years ago a colleague shared the idea of having parents complete an Areas of Expertise (AoE) Survey at the beginning of the school year to identify skills and talents they could share with the class and/or school during the school year. Invite parents and caregivers to do so, and be particularly mindful of the skills and talents that further intercultural understanding.

Family resources

Include articles, books, links to videos, podcasts and other resources that pertain to intercultural understanding in school newsletters, and provide digital and library resources families can use and discuss at home with their children.

Parent Teacher Association (PTA)

Look for ways the PTA can support teaching and learning for intercultural understanding such as bringing in guest speakers, sponsoring trips, supporting initiatives, and planning cultural and language events throughout the year.

Establish a transition team

Many schools establish a transition team to facilitate the arrival and departure of families in the school, and provide transition education and support throughout the school. Consider establishing one at your school. The team usually includes parents, teachers, administrators and students.

Immigrant and refugee families

Be particularly mindful of how the school can reach out and include immigrant and refugee families in social and cultural events. Consider ways to provide language support, and provide opportunities to learn their languages as well. Provide a buddy family for new families, and encourage ways they can volunteer and participate in the life of the school.

Appendix F
Connecting with the community

Schools can build strong bridges to the local community by opening their doors and inviting local residents in, as well as reaching out, and supporting and participating in community events.

- Invite the community in to share in the students' projects that pertain to intercultural understanding, such as art or photography exhibitions, videos and presentations.

- Seek partnerships with local libraries, galleries, theatres and other public spaces to showcase the children's intercultural learning and projects.

- Invite community leaders, speakers and cultural groups into the school to conduct workshops and give presentations.

- Plan field trips to participate in community events that highlight its cultural and linguistic diversity.

- Seek ways children and families can volunteer in the local community. This could support established community efforts or involve new initiatives such as welcoming newcomers and addressing environmental issues.

- Plan events with your students that reach out to immigrant and refugee children. This could be a Games Day where children teach each other a game from their culture, and play international or cooperative games. Children might participate in yoga or mindfulness activities (see *Planting Seeds* in Appendix D). This might take place at your school or a nearby recreation centre.

Appendix G

Organisations that promote intercultural understanding

This is a list of organisations that support and promote intercultural understanding in addition to those in Appendix C. Some are included in both appendices. All websites were accessed in January 2018.

www.kofiannanfoundation.org

This website informs us of the work of the Kofi Annan Foundation to help create a fairer and more peaceful world.

http://asiasociety.org/education/educators

The Asia Society is a global non-profit organisation focused on building understanding between the Asia Pacific region and the West.

www.cal.org and this description:

The Center for Applied Linguistics (CAL) promotes language learning and cultural understanding, and helps facilitate immigrant and refugee integration.

https://facinghistory.org

This website provides excellent background knowledge and materials for secondary school students and educators, many of which can be adapted for primary school.

www.ofeliagarcia.org

Professor Ofelia García's website provides useful publications and articles on translanguaging, bilingualism and education.

www.idrinstitute.org/index.asp

The Intercultural Development Research Institute (IDRInstitute) is an international non-profit organisation that promotes intercultural communication in our multicultural and global world. It showcases the work of Milton Bennett and others, and provides articles related to intercultural learning.

www.oxfam.org.uk

Oxfam works around the world to eradicate poverty and respond to families in crisis.

www.savethechildren.org.uk

This website provides information about the ways Save the Children works to protect the rights of children around the world.

www.unesco.org

This website will inform you of the ongoing work of UNESCO to help promote a peaceful and equitable world.

www.unicef.org

Discover the ways that UNICEF advocates for the rights of children around the globe to protect the life of every child, every day.

www.wateraid.org

WaterAid is working to provide clean water, sanitation and hygiene for all people by 2030. This website informs us of their work and provides information about worldwide initiatives to protect our water resources.

Appendix H
Templates for lesson plans

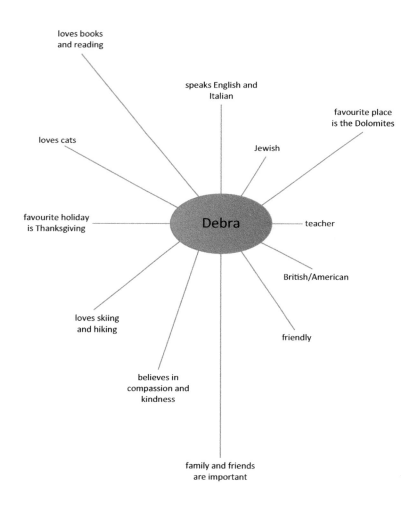

loves books
and reading

speaks English and
Italian

favourite place
is the Dolomites

loves cats

Jewish

favourite holiday
is Thanksgiving

Debra

teacher

British/American

loves skiing
and hiking

friendly

believes in
compassion and
kindness

family and friends
are important

Personal and Cultural Identity Map sample parent letter

Date

Dear Parents,

We will be creating Personal and Cultural Identity Maps at school. Our identity is our sense of who we are and how we see ourselves. It is a combination of our cultures, languages, personal traits, life experiences, values, passions, interests and preferences. Your child has completed an Identity Chart at school and a plan for what to bring from home. Please go over this plan with your child and help him or her gather the photographs and other materials he or she needs to complete this project. Please send them to school with your child by (date).

Many thanks for your help.

With kind regards,

Personal and Cultural Identity Map planning sheet

Use this space to plan your map. You can draw and write your ideas from your identity chart here.

Materials to bring from home:

Materials to find at school:

These might be family and personal photographs, downloaded images, brochures, etc.

Story Behind My Name sample parent letter

Date

Dear Parents,

Our names are deeply meaningful and personal, and are an important part of our identity. We will be exploring the importance, value and meaning of our names, and sharing the origin of our given name(s) in class. There are different reasons names are chosen in different cultures and families, such as family tradition or naming a child after a relative. Could you please talk with your child about the story behind his or her name, and how and why it was chosen? Please have your child write his or her name in the original script as well as English if applicable. You and your child should then complete the sheet below to bring to class on (date).

Many thanks for your help.

With kind regards,

MY NAME _____

My name was chosen because _____

_____

_____

_____

_____

_____

_____

_____

_____

_____

_____

_____

_____

_____

_____

_____

_____

_____

Epilogue: To teachers everywhere

I believe deeply in teachers and all you can achieve, and how you can transform our world for good. And I believe deeply in children and how they, too, can transform our world for good, now and in the future.

When we intentionally help children learn and grow with intercultural understanding we enable them to live rich and fulfilling lives. We help them to develop meaningful human connections. We provide them with the ability to ensure the health and well-being of our planet, and to create the more peaceful, equitable and compassionate world in which we wish to live. Teaching and learning for intercultural understanding has the power to help change lives, and to lift up our communities and each other.

This book is an expression of love and hopefulness. Our world needs you, the children need you, and we all need each other. Our journey is just beginning. And what an exciting journey it is, filled with promise and hope for a better world. I hold all of you in my heart as you teach and inspire our future generations.

Index

accents: stereotypes and 'linguistic profiling' 110–111; in *Amazing Grace* 122

ACORN Foundation and Dharavi Project 186

Ada, A. F. and Zubizarreta G. M.: *Dancing Home* 76–82

adaptability, and managing change 129; and resilience 141

addressing stereotypes, prejudice, discrimination and racism 46, 113–114 and definitions, 136

Adiche, C. N.: 'The Danger of a Single Story' 33

affirming and empowering children 26, 56, 85, 97, 98, 99, 100, 115, 174, 189

Aliki: *Marianthe's Story: Painted Words and Spoken Memories* 152–155

Alliance for International Education (AIE) 2014 Conference on Intercultural Understanding in Mumbai 9, 13, 25, 26

All the Colors We Are: The Story of How We Get Our Skin Color (Kissinger) 122

Amazing Grace (Hoffman) 120–124

American International School of Lusaka (AISL), examples of developing intercultural understanding 185–186

American School of Bombay (ASB), examples of developing intercultural understanding 182–183, 186–187

Annan, Kofi: speech at Tübingen University and universal values 87

anti-bias education 114–115, 119, 201

anticipating and normalising difference 110–111

Appleseed Community Center 189

appreciation and respect for diversity 83, 88–89; our own 34, *The Glitterlings* 44; *see also Amazing Grace; Each Kindness; The Golden Rule; One Green Apple; The Other Side; sharing cultural artefacts; Tokyo Friends/ Tokyo no Tomodachi; What Does It Mean to Be Global? Wish: Wishing Traditions Around the World*

Asia Society (and Council of Chief State School Officers) 12; four global competences 17–18; 21, 158, 196, 204

assimilation, and names 111

assimilation vs. integration 59–60, 116; in *The Name Jar* 63; in *One Green Apple* 125

attitude of awareness 90

attitude of engagement 90

attitude of integrity 90

Australian Curriculum Assessment Reporting Authority (ACARA) and intercultural understanding 1, 12–13, 190 at Westgarth Primary School, Northcote, Victoria 190

Bang, M.: *When Sophie's Feelings Are Really, Really Hurt* 145–147

Barrett, M. et al 39, 47

Because of You (Hennessy) 174–175

beliefs, values and attitudes: a shared understanding of the terms 83; that can transform our lives and world for good 83; to develop intentionally for intercultural understanding 88–90; *see also Each Kindness; The Golden Rule; What Does It Mean to Be Global?*

belief in human rights and dignity for all people 89

belief in social justice and equity 90

belonging and connection 117, 118

benefits of teaching and learning for intercultural understanding 26–27

Bennett, J. 12, 13, 21

Bennett, Milton, and the DMIS 26, 31; and the IDI 32, 36, 204

Berlin Metropolitan School (BMS), examples
of developing intercultural understanding:
home language programme and home
language ambassadors 45; political migration
and integration project 187–188
Beyond Culture (Hall) 41
BIG (Paratore) 175
bilingualism 43, 204; *see also Dancing Home*
Blair, Tracy, ASB, global book club 182
body language 140, 152, 153
body size and shape 89, 115, 178
Bokova, Irina 156
Brooks, David: *The Road to Character* 85; *The
Social Animal* 35
Brown, Brenè: *Daring Greatly: How the Courage
to Be Vulnerable Transforms the Way We
Live, Love, Parent and Lead,* 'fitting in' and
'belonging' 59, 61
building community 4, 173, 175–180, 183
building resilience and managing change 141;
see also resilience; managing change
bullying 25, 113, 194, 195, 197, 201; in
Dancing Home 76, 80; in *Each Kindness* 105,
107, 108; in *The Golden Rule* 95
Bunting, E.: *One Green Apple* 125–130
Byram, M. 42, 47

Cambridge International Examinations 35
caring *see* caring and kindness
caring and kindness 88; *see also* kindness
Castle, C. and UNICEF: *For Every Child: The
rights of the child in words and pictures* 162–164
change *see* managing change
changing demographics 24
character education 84–86
Chicken Sunday (Polacco) 148–151
children at risk 25
Choi, Y.: *The Name Jar* 63–70
Chumak-Horbatsch, Roma Linguistically
Appropriate Practice (LAP) 44; at
Thornwood Public School 189
Claris, Elke, ISS Sindelfingen 188
code-switching 43, 78 in *Dancing Home* 78
collaboration 73, 74, 75, 140, 141, 143, 160, 174,
176, 177; with children 181–182, 183; with
colleagues 180–181; whole-school 181–182;
collaboration and cooperation 140, 141
common humanity 14, 17, 23, 28, 86, 88, 91,
110; *see also* shared values
communication *see* effective communication;
intercultural communication

community building *see* building community
compassion and empathy 88; *see also*
compassion; empathy
compassion: *Just Like Me* activity 113, 197; *see
also* compassion and empathy
confidence *see* confidence and courage;
self-confidence
confidence and courage 89–90, 116, 118; *see
also* courage; self-confidence
conflict resolution 16, 34, 112–113, 139, 140, 158;
in *Chicken Sunday* 149–150; in *Dancing Home*
80; in *Peace Begins with You* 169
Cooper, I.: *The Golden Rule* 93–96
Council of Europe (CoE): framework for
intercultural competence 28
courage 106, 114, 124, 149; *see also Amazing
Grace; Chicken Sunday;* confidence and
courage; *One Green Apple; The Other Side*
creative and critical thinking 140–141
creativity 14, 26, 71, 85, 146, 160, 178, 180
cross-culture kid (CCK): who cross-culture
kids are 57
cross-cultural skills *see* intercultural skills
culture, concept of 39–40; *see sharing cultural
artefacts; Tokyo Friends/Tokyo no Tomodachi;
Wish: Wishing Traditions Around the World*
cultural artefact, sharing 52–53
cultural differences 32, 39, 40, 41, 42, 46, 47,
58, 60; 112, 138, 141, 175, 191; in *Chicken
Sunday* 151; in *Dancing Home* 79; in *When
Sophie's Feelings Are Really, Really Hurt* 146
see also DMIS; *sharing cultural artefacts; Tokyo
Friends/Tokyo no Tomodachi; Wish: Wishing
Traditions Around the World*
cultural iceberg *see* Iceberg Model of Culture
cultural identity *see* personal and cultural
identity
Cummins, Jim 44
cultural intelligence 12, 15, 19
curiosity and interest in others 88
curiosity 1, 14, 15, 88, 97, 102, 110, 115, 46,
158, 160, 161, 175, 181; *see also* curiosity
and interest in others
Cushner, Kenneth 12, 13, 25–26, 113
cyberbullying 25, 194, 197

Dancing Home (Ada and Zubizarreta) 76–82
Danger of a Single Story, The (Adiche) TED Talk
33, 36
Deardorff, D. 12, 14, 21
de Leo, Joy 10, 11, 13, 26

defusing conflict 112

Derman-Sparks, Linda: anti-bias education 114–115

designing learning and living spaces with intercultural understanding in mind 173–179; building community 175; the physical space 176–177; routines, rituals and practices 177–178; setting the tone 173–175;

develop and sustain positive relationships 142; *see also Chicken Sunday; Marianthe's Story: Painted Words and Spoken Memories; When Sophie's Feelings Are Really, Really Hurt*

developing all human potential 27

developing intercultural understanding, and anti-bias education 114; as a lifelong process 30, 33; in children 183–184; in ourselves 34; support for in schools 27–28; l virtues 85

Developmental Model of Intercultural Sensitivity (DMIS) 26; six stages of 31–32, 36

difference: tolerance and respect for 89; *see also* cultural differences; respect for all differences

dignity, human 2, 11, 18, 27, 30, 33, 46, 60, 83, 87, 89, 106, 108, 115, 118

dimensions of culture, Hofstede 41–42

DiOrio, Rana intercultural skills 140; *What Does It Mean to Be. . .?®* series 97; *What Does It Mean To Be Global?* 97–104; *What Does It Meant to Be Kind?* 106; *What Does It Meant To Be Present?* 168; *What Does It Meant to Be Safe?* 163

discrimination 46, 113–114, 115, 118, 136, 191; in *Amazing Grace* and definition for children 120, 121, 124; countering discriminatory behaviours 84; definition 136; in *Each Kindness* 108; in *One Green Apple* 129; in *The Other Side* 132; *see also* addressing stereotypes, prejudice, discrimination and racism

diversity, appreciation and respect for *see* cultural and linguistic diversity 188, 203; *see also* richness and benefits of diversity

DMIS *see* Developmental Model of Intercultural Sensitivity

Does Your Accent Make You Smarter? (Luu Chi) 110

Don't Ask Me Where I'm From, Ask Where I'm a Local (Selasi) TED Talk 58

dual language schools: Berlin Metropolitan School 187; ISS Sindelfingen 188

dual language texts 44 79, 176, 177; dual language migration stories 189

Dut, Salva 166

Each Kindness (Woodson) 105–108

Education 2030 12, 22, 92

education to build bridges and for social change 28

Education for Global Citizenship (Oxfam) 15, 92

Education for Intercultural Understanding (de Leo) 26

Education for Sustainable Development (ESD) 11, 12; goals (SDGs) 156–157, 161

effective communication 113, 137, 139, 145; in *Chicken Sunday* 149; *see also Marianthe's Story: Painted Words and Spoken Memories; When Sophie's Feelings Were Really, Really Hurt*

embedding local and global issues in our schools 158–160

emotional regulation *see* managing emotions

emotions *see* managing emotions

empathy 14, 16, 17, 25, 35, 44, 60, 87, 91, 137, 138, 142, 166, 177, 186, 187; use of simulations to develop 159; *see also Amazing Grace;* compassion and empathy; *Each Kindness; The Golden Rule; One Green Apple; The Other Side; What Does It Mean to Be Global?*

English language learners (ELLs) 44, 175, 189

European Council of International Schools (ECIS) 34

examples of best practice to promote teaching and learning for intercultural understanding 185–191

examples of children developing intercultural understanding 183–184

exploring and managing our emotions 116

eye contact use of 40, 42, 50, 137

Facing History and Ourselves 196

family involvement *see* parents and caregivers

Fanelli, S.: *My Map Book,* personal and cultural identity map project 71–75

fear of difference 24, 116, 132

flexibility 14, 85, 117

flexible learning environment, American School of Bombay 177

For Every Child: The rights of the child in words and pictures (Castle and UNICEF) 162–164

Framework for Developing Intercultural Understanding (Rader) 3, 9, 20, 192

Friedman, Grace, White Center Elementary School 45, 104
friendships and relationships: develop and sustain positive 142; multicultural 118

Gallagher, Eithne 44, 196
Game Rangers International 186
Garcia, Ofelia: dynamic bilingualism, translanguaging 43, 200, 204
gender: accurate images 123, 176; discrimination 113; equality 12, 122, 157; identification 89, 115, 176; prejudice 122; stereotypes 25, 33, 42, 110, 120, 122
gestures, differences in 40, 48, 138, 153
Ghandi, Mahatma 28
global book club 182–183
global citizenship 1, 11–12, 15–17, 20, 23, 27, 89, 97, 100
GCE *see* Global Citizenship Education
Glitterlings, The 44
Global Citizenship Education (GCE) 17, 156, 158
Global Citizenship Education: Topics and Learning Objectives (UNESCO) 17, 197
global competence: Asia Society and Council of Chief State School Officers 17–18; PISA defined 18
Global Futures Initiative 87
globalisation 11, 16, 23, 87
golden rule 87, 174; *see also Golden Rule, The*
Golden Rule, The (Cooper) 93–96
growing support for developing intercultural understanding in schools 27–28

A Handful of Quiet: Happiness in Four Pebbles (Hanh) 142
Hanh, Thich Nhat 142
Hall, Edward T.: iceberg model of culture 40; high and low context cultures, differences in proxemics, and monochronic and polychronic cultures 41
Hattie, John: collaboration 180; *Visible Learning: A Synthesis of Over 800 Meta-Analyses Relating to Achievement* 35, 36
Haworth, Amanda, ISS Sindelfingen 44, 175
Hayden, Mary 28
healthy relationships, effective communication 137
Helping to create a better world (Chapter 12) 185–191
Hoffman, M.: *Amazing Grace* 120–124
Hofstede, Geert 41–42, and six dimensions of culture, 47

home languages and cultures *see* valuing languages and cultures in our classrooms
home language: home language ambassadors 45, 189; home language programmes 45, 189; importance of 43, in *Dancing Home* 78; integrating them in the classroom and life of the school 40; and well-being 43
honouring and preserving all languages 45–46
hope 87, 89, 118, 194, 195; in *The Other Side* 131–136; *see also* optimism
How Children Succeed: Grit, Curiosity and the Hidden Power of Character (Tough) 84
human migration 24
human rights 1, 10, 11, 12, 14, 16, 22, 27, 28, 46, 83, 86, 87, 89, 115, 118, 156, 160, 200; belief in human rights and dignity for all people 89; *see also For Every Child: The rights of the child in words and pictures*
humility 85, 139, 140; cultural humility 14

IB programmes 10–11
iceberg model of culture 40
identity: and enhanced self-esteem and self-confidence 59; *see also* personal and cultural identity
identity texts 44; *see also* dual language texts
IDI *see* Intercultural Development Inventory
ignorance 80, 92, 102, 121, 154
immigrants 24, 57, and assimilation 60, 116; in *Dancing Home* 82, 118; in *One Green Apple* 125, 127 130; in *Marianthe's Story: Painted Words and Spoken Memories* 155
importance of recognising both differences and similarities 109
inclusion 17, 88, 98, 107, 114, 115, 127, 174, 189
inclusive classrooms 25, 35, 63
inflammatory speech, and respect 113
integration, effective and 'reaching in' and 'reaching out' 116, 118, *see also One Green Apple*
integrity 14, 30, 90,113, 140, 158
intentionality: intentional planning 4; intentional teaching and learning 21, 25, 26, 29, 43, 45, 46, 56, 84, 88, 89, 91, 101, 114, 130, 137, 141, 142, 173, 178, 211
intercultural awareness 26, 33, 81 in *Dancing Home*, 138, 140, in *Chicken Sunday* 150, 188, 201
intercultural communication 32, 47, 138, 140, 143, 204, in *Chicken Sunday* 150

intercultural competence 13–14 as a lifelong process 25–26; Council of Europe Framework for 28; skills and competences for 14
Intercultural Competences (UNESCO) 14
Intercultural Development Inventory (IDI) 32, 36
intercultural sensitivity 138
intercultural skills 26, 47, 138–139, 140, 143; *see also* STOP, LOOK, LISTEN AND LEARN strategy
intercultural understanding: as a disposition and competence 9; as a lifelong process 2, 4, 30, 33, 180; description 20; historical context 10–12; in the Australian Curriculum 1, 12–13
interest inventory 177
interlingual teaching and learning 44; at ISS Sindelfingen 188, 196
International Baccalaureate (IB) 2, 92; history, mission and programmes 10–11
International Baccalaureate Primary Years Programme (IBPYP) 14–15, 20, 21, 28, 45, 158
International Commission on Education for the Twenty-first Century (UNESCO) 11
international education 2, 10, 11, 20, 21, 28
international-mindedness 14–15; in an internationally-minded school 35; in the IBPYP, in the IPC; in 21st century teachers 34
International Primary Curriculum (IPC) 15, 21
International School of Dusseldorf (ISD) Water and Food for Somalia Project 159–160
International School of Florence: L'Aquila aid project 87; WaterAid project 184
International School of Stuttgart Sindelfingen Sindelfingen (ISS Sindelfingen), examples of developing intercultural understanding 44, 175, 188–189
International Teacher Certificate (ITC) skills for 21st century teachers 34–35
internationally mobile children *see* Third Culture Kids (TCKs)
interpersonal skills 139–140, 142; conflict resolution 140; listening and questioning 139; observing and responding 140
intolerance for difference 23

Jagland, Thorbjørn 28
Jubilee Centre for Character and Virtues, University of Birmingham 84–85, 92, 196; framework for character education 85

Kavelin, J. 85
Kavelin-Popov, L. 85
Kehelland Village School 85–86, 92, 141
Kids Random Acts of Kindness 106
kindness 35, 83, 85, 86, 87, 90, 102, 115, 116, 168, 174, 178, 197; *What Does It Mean to Be Kind?* 106; *see also Amazing Grace;* caring and kindness; *Each Kindness; The Golden Rule; One Green Apple; The Other Side; What Does It Mean to Be Global?*
kindness.org 86
Kissinger, Kate: *All the Colors We Are: The Story of How We Get Our Skin Color* 122
Kline, J. M. 87, Global Futures Initiative 2015
knowing ourselves 31–33

language: and identity 42–43; integrating home languages in the classroom and life of the school 4; language differences 10; pedagogy 40–45; *see* honouring and preserving all languages; valuing languages and cultures in our classrooms
language learning and intercultural understanding 194
LAP *see* Linguistically Appropriate Practice
leadership: developing leadership in children 86, 90, 91, 141, 161, 168, 184, 190
learning differences 115, 175
learning logs, for students 69, 142; for teachers 3
LGBTQ 89, 115
life skills 140–142
lifelong learners: ourselves as 34–35; students as 11, 15, 88
Linguistically Appropriate Practice (LAP) 44–45; at Thornwood Public School 189
link between language and culture 42–43
listening 14, 35, 112, 137, 138; reflective listening139
listening and questioning 139 *see also* listening; questioning
local and global issues 27; human rights, water as a resource and peace; *see For Every Child: The rights of the child in words and pictures; One Well; Peace Begins with You*
A Long Walk to Water (Park) 166, 193, 198
Luu, Chi 110, 119

MacDonald, Helen *H is for Hawk*: interview on NPR and otherness 117–118
making a positive difference: helping to create a better world 185–191; *see also Each Kindness;*

The Golden Rule; What Does It Mean to Be Global?
managing change 82, 141
managing emotions 112, 147, 168, 169; and mindfulness 116, 142; our emotions 30, 35, 124; *see also Dancing Home;* exploring and managing our emotions; *One Green Apple; The Other Side; When Sophie's Feelings Are Really, Really Hurt*
Mandela, Nelson 117
Marama, Andrew, ASB, 184, 187
March 4th 97
Marianthe's Story: Painted Words and Spoken Memories (Aliki) 152–155
mediation, peer 112
meeting local and global challenges 1, 23, 27, 29, 135, 156, 158, 159, 161, 169, 178, 184
Melbourne Declaration on Education Goals for Young Australians 158
mental health 25; *see also* well-being
Mindful Movements: Ten Exercises for Well-Being (Hahn) 142
mindfulness 52, 68, 90, 116, 142, 147, 168, 197; and intentionality 173, 178; and managing emotions 142; and self-esteem
mobility *see* transition
Model of Transition Education 56
modelling, for children 4, 20, 28, 35, 46, 84, 88, 91, 111, 112, 115, 118, 138, 140, 143, 175, 180, 181
multicultural: homes, schools, communities 1, 27, 57, 60, 111, 118, 176, 181, 197, 204; identity 57, 158, 175; *see Amazing Grace; One Green Apple; The Other Side*
multilingualism 15, 34, 43, 47, 78; at Thornwood Public School 189, 190
multiple perspectives 13, 14, 178
Mumbai 9, 21
Murphy, Owen ISS Sindelfingen 188
My Map Book (Fanelli), personal and cultural identity map 71–75

Name Jar, The (Choi) 63–70
names: as part of our identity; assimilation and; importance of valuing our
names 111; pronouncing names correctly 111, 175; *see also Dancing Home; Marianthe's Story: Painted Words and Spoken Memories; The Name Jar; Story Behind My Name* project

New Kid in School: Using Literature to Help Children in Transition (Rader and Sittig) 56, 57, 117, 142, 159, 199
news, credibility 127
NGOs 176; and ASB, Mumbai 186–187
nonverbal behaviour *see* body language

observing and responding 140, 143
OECD PISA *see* Organisation for Economic Co-operative Development Programme for International Student Assessment
Olsen Edwards, Julie, anti-bias education 114–115
One Green Apple (Bunting) 125–130
One! International 187
One Well: The Story of Water on Earth (Strauss) 165–166
open-mindedness 88
optimism *see* hope; optimism and belief that we can make a positive difference
optimism and the belief that we can make a positive difference 89; *see also* hope
Organisation for Economic Co-operation and Development Programme for International Student Assessment (OECD PISA), and test for global competence 18
Other Side, The (Woodson) 131–136
our changing world 23–24
Oxfam 11, 12, 15–17, 158

P21 framework; mission 28
Panter-Brick, Catherine: resilience 141
parents and caregivers, working with 4, 5, 25, 35, 41, 42, 45, 58, 61, 74, 111, 112, 173, 174, 175, 194, 197, 199, 200–201; including in learning 53, 123, 177
peace 23, 34, 47, 87, 110, 112, 157, 169, 195, 204–205; and Education 2030 12; and global citizenship education 17; and IB programmes 14; role of education in the UNDHR and UNCRC 10, 112, 113 *see also For Every Child: The rights of the child in words and pictures; Peace Begins with You*
Peace Begins with You (Scholes) 167–169
pedagogy that promotes home languages 43–46
peer mediation 112
personal and cultural identity: how it is shaped 57–58; link to self-esteem and self-confidence 59, what it is and its importance 56

Personal and Cultural Identity Map project, *My Map Book* (Fanelli) 71–75

physical and learning differences 115, 176

Planting Seeds: Practicing Mindfulness with Children (Hanh) 142

Polacco, P.: *Chicken Sunday* 148–151

Pollock, D. 57, 61, 199

Popov, D. 85

Powell, William: power of the pause, and listening skills 139

Power of Connection (Schleifer) TED Talk 109, 118, 119

plastics in our water 156, 166

prejudice 25, 32, 35, 46, 82, 113–114, 115, 118, 136, 197; in *Amazing Grace* and definition for children 120, 121, 124; in *Dancing Home* 80; definition 136; in *Each Kindness* 108; as a learned response 32; in *The Other Side* 132; *see also* addressing stereotypes, prejudice, discrimination and racism

problem-solving 14, 139, 140; problem-solving and decision-making 140, 141, 146

professional development 32, 35, 75

Programme for International Schools Assessment (PISA) 18; bullying and well-being 25; test for global competence 2018 18, 27

questioning 74, 139, 140, 143, 153, 158, 169, 183

racism 1, 23, 25, 46, 81, 84, 104, 113–114, 131, 135, 136, 197; in *Amazing Grace* and definition for children 120, 121, 124; definition 136; in *The Other Side* 135; *see also* addressing stereotypes, prejudice, discrimination and racism

Rader, D. *Framework for Developing Intercultural Understanding* 3, 9, 19–20, 192

Rader, D. *Valuing Languages and Cultures: The First Step Towards Intercultural Understanding* 9, 22, 23, 2,173, 178

Rader, D. and Sittig, L.: *New Kid in School: Using Literature to Help Children in Transition* 40, 46, 56, 57, 58, 117, 138, 141, 142, 159, 199

'reaching in' and 'reaching out' 80, 116–117, 118, 125, 128, in Berlin Metropolitan School political migration and integration project 187–188, what it might look like 116–117

recognising our own stereotypes and prejudice 32–33

ReDI School 187–188

reflection as an essential skill for intercultural understanding 16, 118; in *Dancing Home* 77, 81; in *Each Kindness* 106; in *The Golden Rule* 94; in *Marianthe's Story: Painted Words and Spoken Memories* 153; in *The Name Jar* 66, 67, 68; in *One Green Apple* 128; in *Peace Begins with You* 168; in *What Does It Mean to Be Global?* 101, 104

reflective practice 4, 15, 142; our practice 26, 30–36

refugees 24, 57, 60, in *Dancing Home* 82, 116; in *Marianthe's Story: Painted Words and Spoken Memories 155,* 166, 187, 188; in *One Green Apple 125,* 127, 130; 141

Reggio Emilia approach to learning 176

Reimers, Fernando et al. *World Course* 27–28

relationships, educating for 24

religion: and the golden rule 87; and identity 58; learning about 45; openness to

religions and beliefs 34; as part of culture 39; right to one's own religion 10, 86; valuing different religions and beliefs 111; world religions at ISS Sindelfingen 188–189; *see also The Golden Rule; One Green Apple; sharing cultural artefacts; Tokyo Friends/Tokyo no Tomodachi; What Does It Mean to Be Global?; Wish: Wishing Traditions Around the World*

religious intolerance 130

resilience 25, 31, 141, 153

respect for all differences 115; modelling your own 175; setting the tone 174

responding 28, 140, 143

responsibility 2, 13, 16, 20, 28, for student learning and well-being 31, for 'reaching in' and 'reaching out' 116; for UNCRC 7; 160; freedom of speech and responsibility 113; *see also Amazing Grace; Each Kindness; For Every Child: The rights of the child in words and pictures; The Golden Rule; One Green Apple; The Other Side;* responsibility for oneself, others and the environment; *What Does It Mean to Be Global?*

responsibility for oneself, others and the environment 89

Reynolds, B.: *Tokyo Friends/Tokyo no Tomodachi 48–51*

richness and benefits of diversity 26

Road to Character, The (Brooks) 85

Roots and Wings: Affirming Culture and Preventing Bias in Early Childhood (York) 115

Sanders, Ella Frances: *Lost in Translation: An Illustrated Compendium of Untranslatable Words From Around the World* 43, 47
Schleicher, Andreas 27
Schleifer, Hedy: *The Power of Connection* TEDxTelAviv Talk 109, 118, 119
Scholes, K.: *Peace Begins with You* 167–169
la Scuola Primaria di Monte San Quirico, whole school collaboration 181–182
segregation *see The Other Side*
Selasi, T. *Don't Ask Me Where I'm From, Ask Where I'm a Local,* TED Talk 58, 62, 200
self-awareness 3, 14, 16, 56, 58, 61, 113, 115 in *Amazing Grace* G 122, in *The Other Side* 132, 136
self-confidence 26, 59, 61, 89–90
self-competence 89
self-esteem and self-confidence 17, 59, 61
self-knowledge 113; students 75; teachers 3, 26
shared values 2, 23, 42, 86, 87, 88, 91, 110 *see also* common humanity
sharing cultural artefacts 52–53
sharing our stories: my story and your story 30–31
skills *see* intercultural skills; interpersonal skills; life skills
Smith, Geoff: Kehelland Village School 141; Primary Curriculum for Character Education 85
Snel, E. *Sitting Still Like a Frog* 142
Social Animal, The (Brooks) 35
social and emotional learning 25, 116, 180
social justice: and education for global citizenship 16; translanguaging to ensure 43, 194, 197; *see also The Golden Rule*; *Each Kindness*; social justice and equity; *What Does It Mean to Be Global?*
socioeconomic status 25, 33, 40, 89, 113, 115, 116, 176
stereotypes 13, 14, 25, 33, 35, 46, 82, 110, 113–114, 115, 118, 119, 136, 176, 191, 194; in *Amazing Grace and definition for children* 120, 121, 124; in *Dancing Home* 80; definition 136; in *Each Kindness* 108; in *The Other Side* 132; recognising our own 32, 33; *see also* addressing stereotypes, prejudice, discrimination and racism
STOP, LOOK, LISTEN and LEARN strategy 138–139

Story Behind My Name project 180–181
Strauss, R.: *One Well: The Story of Water on Earth* 165–166
Sustainable Development Goals: 2030 Agenda 156–157, 161
sustainability 1, 11, 84, 156–158; at Westgarth Primary School 158, 190

Tang, Qian 156
teachers as powerful role models 35
teaching of values in schools 84–86
Teaching Tolerance 96,
Teaching Tolerance Anti-Bias Framework K-12 115, 119, 197
technology: balanced use of 4–5; expanding technology 23; to foster global connections 183, 199
Tetley, Ana, ISD 26, 159, 160
Third Culture Kids (TCKs) 57
Thompson, Jeff 28
Thong, R.: *Wish: Wishing Traditions Around the World* 54–55
Thornwood Public School (TPS), celebrating religious diversity and inclusion 189; examples of developing intercultural understanding 189-190; home language programme 45; language ambassadors 189; Linguistically Appropriate Practice (LAP) 189; welcoming immigrants and refugees 189
Tips for Teachers *see* Introduction 4–5
Tokyo Friends/Tokyo no Tomodachi (Reynolds) 48–51
tolerance 10, 14, 27, 80, 85, 90, 108, 112, 113, 115, 130; religious tolerance 129; teaching tolerance 96
tolerance and respect for difference 89
Tough, Paul: *How Children Succeed: Grit, Curiosity and the Hidden Power of Character* 84
transition 56, 138, 141, 177, establish a transition team 202; in *Dancing Home* 116, 117; *see also* mobility; Model for Transition Education; welcoming new students
translanguaging 43, 44, 47, 78, 177, 200, 204
trauma 25, 117
trust 25, 36, 118, 191
Tyler, Julie, ISD 159

UN Global Goals for Sustainable Development 27
United Nations Convention on the Rights of the Child (UNCR) 10, 27, 43, 86, 91, 162–164; child friendly version 163

United Nations Declaration of Human Rights
(UNDHR) 86, 91, role of education in
developing intercultural understanding 10
United Nations Education Science and
Curriculum Organisation (UNESCO)
10, 14, 197, 205; education for sustainable
development 156; global citizenship education
11–12, 17, 88, 130, 158; tolerance 130
UNCRC see United Nations Convention on
the Rights of the Child
UNDHR see United Nations Declaration of
Human Rights
UNESCO see United Nations Education
Science and Curriculum Organisation
universal values see Annan, Kofi, common
humanity; shared values

values: living aligned with our values 91;
see also shared values; teaching of values
in schools
Values Based Education (VbE) 85
valuing languages and cultures in our
classrooms 45, 173, 178, 188
Van Reken, Ruth 57, 62, 199
Virtues Project, The 85–86, and building
resilience 141, virtues for developing
intercultural understanding 85

water as a global issue: plastics in 156, 166;
scarcity 159, 165, 166; see One Well
Water and Food for Somalia Project 159–160
We Dine Together 107, 195
welcoming new students, in Each Kindness 106;
in The Golden Rule 94; in The Name Jar 68;
in One Green Apple 128

Welcoming Schools 115, 119, 198
well-being 18, 25, 29, 33, 43, 59, 84, 116,
118, 157, 178, 199; and mindfulness 142,
of society and our planet 161; 144; outdoor
learning and 159;
Westgarth Primary School, celebrating diversity
191; examples of developing intercultural
understanding 158, 190–191; language and
culture 190; sustainability 158
What Does It Mean to Be. . .?® series 97
What Does It Mean to Be Global? (Year 3–Year 6)
(DiOrio) 100–104
What Does It Mean to Be Kind? (DiOrio) 106
What Does It Mean to Be Present? (DiOrio) 168
What Does It Mean to Be Safe? (DiOrio) 163
When Sophie's Feelings Are Really, Really Hurt
(Bang) 145–147
White Center Heights Elementary School,
examples of developing intercultural
understanding 45, 104
white privilege 113, 119
whole school collaboration, la Scuola Primaria
di Monte San Quirico 181–182
Wish: Wishing Traditions Around the World
(Thong) 54–55
Woodson, J.: Each Kindness 105–108; Other
Side, The 131–136
World Course: global citizenship education
curriculum 27

xenophobia 23, 84

York, Stacey: anti-bias education 115; racism
113; Roots and Wings: Affirming Culture and
Preventing Bias in Early Childhood 115

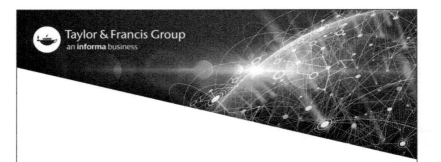